Mustang
1964½–1970

INTERIOR
Restoration Guide

Art Trantafello

MOTORBOOKS
INTERNATIONAL

First published in 1986 by Motorbooks International, an
imprint of MBI Publishing Company, Galtier Plaza, Suite 200,
380 Jackson Street, St. Paul, MN 55101-3885 USA

The information in this book is true and complete to the best of
our knowledge. All recommendations are made without any
guarantee on the part of the author or Publisher, who also
disclaim any liability incurred in connection with the use of this
data or specific details.

We recognize that some words, model names, and designations
mentioned herein are the property of the trademark holder. We
use them for identification purposes only. This is not an official
publication.

Motorbooks International titles are also available at discounts in
bulk quantity for industrial or sales-promotional use. For details
write to Special Sales Manager at Motorbooks International
Wholesalers & Distributors, Galtier Plaza, Suite 200,
380 Jackson Street, St. Paul, MN 55101-3885 USA.

ISBN 0-87938-211-2

Printed in USA

Contents

Preface

This book was written to help you reupholster your Ford Mustang in a professional way. Some of the questions probably on your mind right now are: Can I do it? Will it really look as good as a professional shop job? How much money can I save? Why should I do it?

If you can use a screwdriver, a pair of pliers, a socket set and the basic home mechanic's tools, then you can do it. And if you follow the step-by-step instructions, there is no reason your job cannot look and be as good as, if not better than, that of most professional shops.

You should be able to save more than fifty percent of the cost of having the work professionally done. Again, the main reason for doing the job yourself is a savings of better than fifty percent. Another reason for doing the job yourself is the pride and satisfaction you will receive and, in many instances, the reward of taking the extra time to do the job a little bit better.

You want to know how *you* can do the job as good as, or better than, a professional, right? Let's look at the facts. A manufacturer spends a lot of time and money to duplicate the correct colors and grain of material, to purchase the proper machines to do the exact stitching (for example, double-needle machines to keep the stitching on the French seams perfect) and to buy heat sealing machines and dies to duplicate the designs on the door panels, the embossed patterns on the back of the front backrest, the embossed Pony inserts and so on. Even some of the best professional, established shops in the country do not have this equipment available to them and, in many instances, cannot even come close to matching the colors or grains of materials used originally on the Mustang. (A good source book is the *Mustang Parts and Services Directory*, which covers 1964½ to 1973 vehicles. It is regularly updated and is cross-referenced in alphabetical, geographical and subject category listings.) Most shops that upholster Mustangs will buy the same kits available to you.

Chapter 1

How to reupholster the seats

There are five basic steps to reupholstering the seats: removing, stripping, preparing, re-covering and installing. (Fig. 1-1).

Here is a list of tools and supplies you will need.

> Phillips screwdriver
> Straight screwdriver (long or heavy-duty)
> 3/8 inch drive socket set
> ½ inch deep-well socket
> Pair of diagonal side cutters
> Pair of hog-ring pliers
> Pair of shears
> ½ pound of hog-rings (more than enough)

Before you begin to work on your Mustang, disconnect the battery so you won't run it down with the interior lights on. Also, always use jack stands while working under the car.

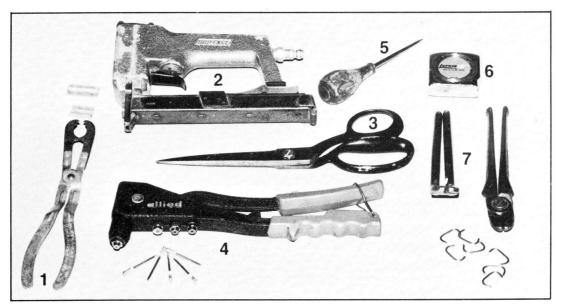

Fig. 1-1. These are some of the special trim tools not usually found in most mechanic's toolboxes but needed to do upholstery work: (1) door handle remover 1964½-65; (2) air staple gun; (3) trimmers, shears; (4) pop-rivet gun and rivets; (5) scratch awl; (6) tape measure; (7) hog-ring pliers, curved and straight, and hog-rings. (Jeff Tann/Argus Publishers Corporation)

Step 1: Removing

Front seat

All coupe, convertible and fastback models are identical for front seat removal. Jack up the car on one side and install jack stands. Directly under the front bucket seat are four rubber plugs; remove them with a straight screwdriver (Fig. 1-2). Next, use a ½ inch deep-well socket with a four- or five-inch extension to remove the four nuts holding the bucket seat in place (the Mustang has a double-thick floor pan; be careful not to lose the nuts between the floor pan). If your car has a bench seat, it will have only two nuts on either side. Repeat this procedure on the opposite side of the car.

Lift out both front seats or the bench seat. Take out the slotted plates that sit on top of the carpet to keep the track from catching the carpet while the seats move forward and backward. These should be cleaned and painted black.

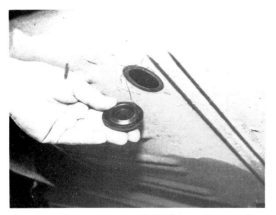

Fig. 1-2. *After removing the rubber plugs under the seat bolts the half-inch nuts holding the seat in place will be exposed.*

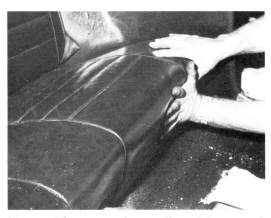

Fig. 1-3. *The rear cushion will not lift out until you push back on the seat and clear the safety catch.*

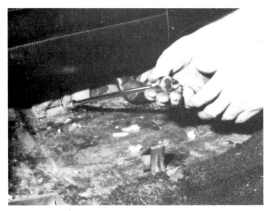

Fig. 1-4. *After removing the rear cushion, the bolts holding the rear backrest in place must be removed.*

Fig. 1-5. *The rear backrest must be lifted before it can be removed.*

Lower the car and you are ready to remove the back seat. Coupe and convertible rear seat removal is the same; only the fastback is different.

Coupe and convertible rear cushion

Push back on the front of the rear cushion, lifting at the same time (Fig. 1-3), until you clear the safety catch holding the rear seat in place. Next, pull the rear seat out toward the front of the car.

Coupe and convertible rear backrest

Use a 3/8 inch socket with a medium-to-long extension to remove the two bolts at the bottom of the rear backrest (Fig. 1-4). Gently lift the backrest about two inches (Fig. 1-5) until it clears the catches at the top. Then pull the backrest forward (this should be done carefully so that you do not damage the headlining while raising the backrest).

Fastback rear cushion

Lift the front edge of the cushion and pull it forward six to eight inches. Push the seat belt ends through the opening in the cushion until they are free. Pull the seat forward and remove it from the car.

Fastback rear backrest

Reach under the metal frame holding the backrest in place and locate the two Phillips screws in the bottom edge of the frame. Remove the two screws and pull the bottom of the backrest out until the two metal tabs are clear. Lift the backrest until the two clamps on the frame are free of the spring unit. Remove the backrest from the car.

Step 2:   Stripping
Buckets

Place the two front bucket seats on a table or work bench. Use a Phillips screwdriver to remove the three screws holding the chrome moldings to the side of the frontrest (Fig. 1-6). Be careful not to lose the

Fig. 1-6. Removing the outside chrome trim is the first step in stripping the seats.

Fig. 1-7. Remove the plastic inside trim to expose the hairpin retaining clips holding the front backrest to the front cushion.

plastic spacers that fit under the chrome. Next, remove the one screw holding the plastic trim piece on the opposite side (Fig. 1-7). Remove the two retaining clips holding the backrest to the cushion (Fig. 1-8). Using a large or heavy-duty screwdriver, pry the outside (longer) arm off the pin and slide the inside arm off the opposite pin (Fig. 1-9). While doing this, note the difference between the driver's cushion and backrest and the passenger's cushion and backrest. If you are unsure of how the listing hold-downs are placed, do one front cushion and one front backrest at a time so that you can see how to attach the listing hold-down.

Lay both cushions face down and carefully remove the spring that pulls the seat forward on the track (Fig. 1-10). Slide both tracks forward (Fig. 1-11) and remove the rear Phillips screws holding the seat to the

Fig. 1-9. The outside arm should be removed first. Always use padding when removing or installing so you don't damage the upholstery on the front cushion.

Fig. 1-8. Use side cutters to remove the hairpin retaining clips.

Fig. 1-10. Note location of spring that moves seat track and remove it before seat track is removed.

Fig. 1-11. Seat track must be pulled forward to expose Phillips screws holding seat track to frame.

bottom of the seat base. Slide the tracks to the rear and remove the two front Phillips screws. Next, carefully remove the seat adjustment mechanism and the tracks from the bottom of the seat (Fig. 1-12). Note that the tracks are identical on both driver's and passenger's cushions; therefore, they are interchangeable. The only track that is different is that on the early-model 1964½ passenger seat, which does not move forward or backward.

Now is a good time to clean, repaint and put a light coat of grease on the track; also paint the spring and seat-adjustment mechanism semigloss black.

Front bucket cushions

Turn the two front seat cushions face side up and remove the two Phillips screws holding a plastic stop at the two rear outside corners of each cushion. After you remove each plastic stop, replace both screws so you can locate them after the new cover is installed (Fig. 1-13). Turn the cushion face down and use your diagonal side cutters to cut the hog-rings loose that hold the seat cover to the seat frame (Fig. 1-14). Pull out

Fig. 1-12. Twist the seat track and remove the seat-adjusting mechanism.

Fig. 1-13. Install the screws into the holes so they can be located later.

Fig. 1-14. Use side cutters to cut old hog-rings to remove upholstery.

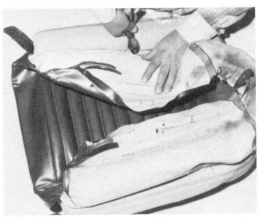

Fig. 1-15. After rolling the old cover over to the insert, cut the hog-rings loose around the insert.

the wire and be sure to save it. Carefully roll the rear corners up over the frame, then roll the two sides and front over the foam and frame.

Turn the seat cushion over. If your car is a 1965, 1966, 1968 or 1969 with standard upholstery, it will have the horseshoe insert on the cushion. If your car has a Pony interior or is a 1967 model it will have two vertical listings and one horizontal listing. The 1969 deluxe and all 1970 standard models have two vertical listings. All the 1968 and 1969 standard seats are identical. All the inserts are held down with hog-rings.

Again, using your diagonal side cutters, cut the hog-rings loose along the inserts and remove the cover (Fig. 1-15). Repeat this procedure on the other cushion. Be sure to save the wires, as you will have to install them in the new covers.

Front bucket backrests

Lay the two front backrests face down on a work table. Using a straight screwdriver, locate the clips holding the backboard in place and remove the backboard from the front backrests (Fig. 1-16). Along-side the longer arm you will see a chrome-plated, ½ inch bolt with a chrome-plated washer and nut. This bolt adjusts the height of the front backrest and sits on the plastic stop that was held to the front cushion with the Phillips screws. Loosen the nut and remove the bolt (Fig. 1-17).

Cut the hog-rings loose around the back edge of the front backrest. Carefully roll the cover back over the foam and you will again see the insert held in place with listing and hog-rings. Cut the hog-rings loose and remove the cover from the front backrest. If your car is a 1965, 1966, 1967, 1968 or 1969 with standard interior, it will have the horse-shoe insert on the front backrest. The 1969 standard and deluxe front backrests had removable headrests; the Mach 1 was the first model to offer highback seats. All the 1970 models had highbacks. However, if

Fig. 1-16. The clips holding the rear panel in place can be popped out with a long straight screwdriver.

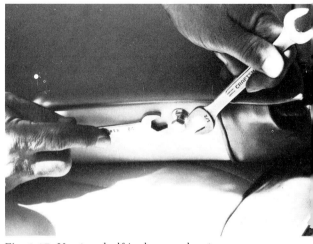

Fig. 1-17. Use two half-inch wrenches to remove the front backrest adjusting bolt. The nut locks it in place and the bolt sets the height.

your car has the Pony interior it will have an insert similar to the 1967 cushion.

Front bench seats

If you are re-covering a bench seat you will notice an extra interior listing on the inside section under the center armrest. This must also be cut loose.

Other than the inside listing under the center armrest, the front bench cushion is identical to all other front cushions. And the only difference between the front rests is that the bucket front rest has two metal arms to attach it to the seat and the bench front rest has one metal arm on the outside and one metal pin on the inside that fits into the armrest mechanism.

Rear cushion

Lay the cushion face down and, using the diagonal side cutters, cut all the hog-rings loose (Fig. 1-18). Remove the wire and pull the cover over the two front corners, then turn the seat right-side up. Continue pulling the two side corners over the padding until you come to the listing holding the wires on either side of the center hump of the cushion. Cut the hog-rings (Fig. 1-19) loose and remove the wires and cover. Be sure to save the wires, as you will need to reuse them for the installation.

Rear backrest

Lay the rear backrest face down (Fig. 1-20), cut all the hog-rings loose, remove the wire (Fig. 1-21) and pull the material over the two top

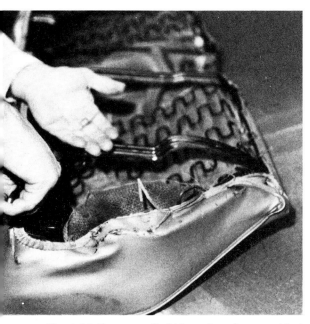

Fig. 1-18. Remove all old hog-rings from seat but keep them off work table. This prevents damage to new upholstery.

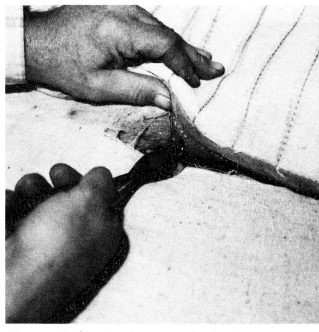

Fig. 1-19. Cut hog-rings loose on each side of rear cushion humps.

corners. Turn the backrest over and remove the cover from the pad. Again, save the wires.

This procedure is the same on all 1964½ through 1970 models.

Step 3: Preparing

Now is the time to show you how to do a more thorough job than most professionals. If you've ever looked under a Mustang seat and seen powdered foam particles and wondered how to eliminate them, here is the answer. The seat frames are covered with burlap; after many years of use, the burlap deteriorates and causes the foam to break down and fall between the springs. This is the ideal time to cut the hog-rings and remove all the foam padding, the horseshoe hold-down wire and the burlap from the seat frames (Fig. 1-22). Using regular mechanic's pliers, tighten all the clips holding the springs to the frame. Next, paint all the seat frames with a black rust-inhibiting enamel spray paint. After the paint is dry, re-cover the seat frames with new burlap.

The rear backrest and rear cushion are relatively simple to work on, but the front backrest and front cushion must have the horseshoe

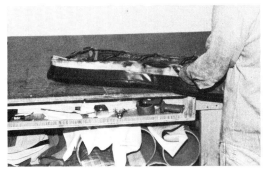

Fig. 1-20. *Stripping a rear backrest is made easier on a work bench.*

Fig. 1-21. *After removing all hog-rings slide wires out of listing for re-use.*

Fig. 1-22. *All old burlap must be removed from frame.*

Fig. 1-23. *Install insert hold-down wire on top of new burlap.*

hold-down wire hog-ringed on top of the burlap in order to hold down the inserts (Fig. 1-23). Next, replace the padding and foam on the top of the burlap and you will be ready to install the covers. If the foam pieces are badly worn or deteriorated, you should consider replacing them with new molded-foam buns available through your local Mustang specialty shop (Fig. 1-24).

Step 4: Re-covering

Remove the upholstery kit from the box and check the pieces (Fig. 1-25). If you have bucket seats, you should have two front cushions, two front backrests, one rear cushion, one rear backrest and two new

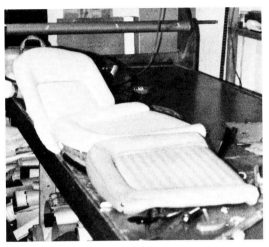

Fig. 1-24. New foam toppers are available.

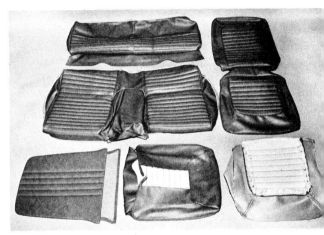

Fig. 1-25. This reproduction seat cover kit is for a 1965 fastback. (Jeff Tann/Argus Publishers Corporation)

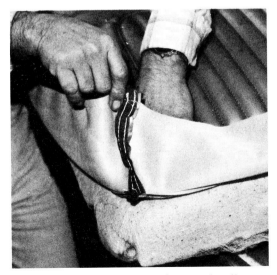

Fig. 1-26. Hold corner in place and roll new cover in position with opposite hand.

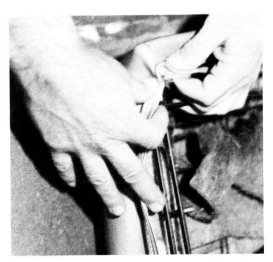

Fig. 1-27. Line up French seam with corner before hog-ringing into place.

covered panel boards with the embossing for the back of the front backrest. If you have a bench seat you will have one front cushion, instead of two, two front backrest pieces (identical to the bucket seat backrests) and a center armrest cover.

The covers are easier to install and the wrinkles come out more easily when the vinyl is warm. A good tip is to leave the covers out in the sun for about a half hour (or, if you don't live in sunny California, room temperature will do).

Rear backrest

Starting with the rear backrest, insert the wires and place the cover on top of the padding. One at a time, roll the upper corners over the seat frame (Fig. 1-26). Next, roll the two lower corners over the frame and turn the backrest face down. Check to see that the French seams (Fig. 1-27) are lined up with the upper corners of the frame.

Starting in the center at the top, hog-ring the upholstery in place. Next, go to the bottom, start in the center and work your way out, in

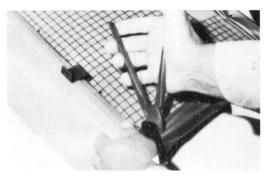

Fig. 1-28. Hog-ring sides of fastback rear backrest after top and bottom are fastened.

Fig. 1-29. Finished 1965 rear backrest looks great.

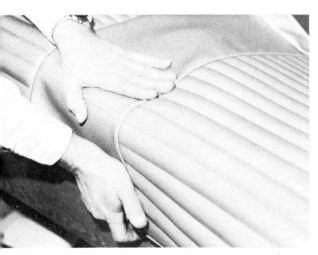

Fig. 1-30. Locate rear cushion position before hog-ringing.

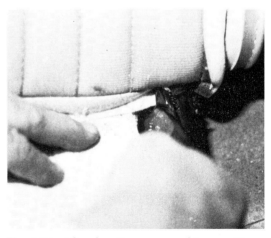

Fig. 1-31. After locating rear cushion position, lift each side and hog-ring wires on each side of hump.

each direction. Hog-ring the bottom (Fig. 1-28). Finish off both sides and this cover is complete (Fig. 1-29).

Rear cushion

Insert wires; don't forget the two wires on either side of the hump. Lay the cover on top of the padding and position the two front corners in place. This helps line up the French seam with the leading edge of the cushion (Fig. 1-30). Next, raise one side and hog-ring the listing on that side of the hump (Fig. 1-31). Lay this side back in place, raise the other side and hog-ring it (Fig. 1-32). (Hog-rings should always catch and fasten the listing wire to the seat frames. The seat frames have slots or cutouts for the hog-rings to go into. The hog-rings do not pierce the foam.)

Now that the hump is fastened in place, check the seams at the two front corners to make sure they are properly positioned and the driveshaft cutout is properly centered. Hog-ring the front edge of the cushion first, then hog-ring the rear section of the cushion in place and finish both sides (Fig. 1-33). Turn the rear cushion over and it is complete (Fig. 1-34).

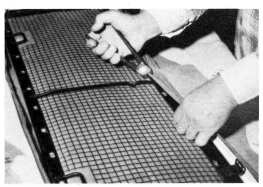

Fig. 1-32. Hog-ringing fastback rear backrest in place is precision work.

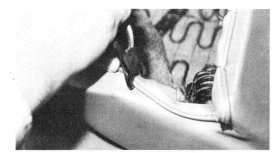

Fig. 1-33. Hog-ring both sides of rear cushion after front and rear are hog-ringed into place.

Fig. 1-34. Rear backrest and rear cushion completed.

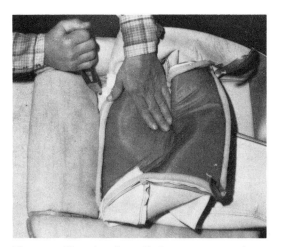

Fig. 1-35. Hog-ring front listing on Pony cushion before hog-ringing both outside listings.

Front cushion

First, insert all wires and lay the cover on top of the padding and seat frame. Check the position to make sure the insert is properly located. Holding the horseshoe insert in place, raise the front edge of the cover and hog-ring the center of the listing to the listing hold-down. Work from side to side of the center and go around the horseshoe until the insert is fastened in place. On a 1967 or a Pony interior, hog-ring the horizontal listing in place first (Fig. 1-35), then hog-ring the vertical listing on each side. On models with vertical pleats only, hog-ring the center listings first and work toward the outside.

Carefully roll the two front corners over the padding but not over the frame yet (Fig. 1-36). Next, roll the two rear corners over the padding and turn the cushion face down. Pull the material over the frame and hog-ring the front in place. Next, hog-ring the rear portion of the cushion, then hog-ring the two sides last. Carefully cut around the pins that hold the backrest in place.

Locate the four holes that hold the track in place and cut a hole just big enough so that the material does not get caught in the threads. Place the track in position and be sure to put the release mechanism in place. Move both tracks forward and install the rear screws loosely in place; slide the tracks back and install the two front screws. Tighten all four screws holding the track. Check the seat-adjustment mechanism so that both tracks will move forward and backward, and still lock in place. Install the springs that slide the tracks back.

Next, turn the cushion over, locate the two screws that hold the stop-plate in place and remove them. Then install the plastic stop-plate and your cushion is complete (Fig. 1-37).

Front backrest

Place the old wire or wires, depending on which model you are doing, into the new listing on the front backrest cover. Position the

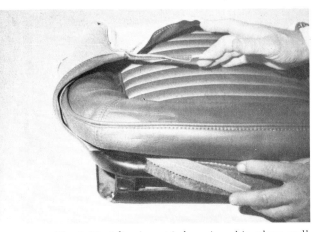

Fig. 1-36. *After insert is hog-ringed in place, roll front corners over foam and hog-ring rear and sides.*

Fig. 1-37. *Completed front cushion should look like this.*

cover on the padding. On the Pony interior, position the cover properly in place and hog-ring the horizontal listing at the upper and lower sides of the Pony insert. Next, hog-ring the two vertical listings on either side of the Pony insert (Fig. 1-38). If your car has the horseshoe insert, position the seat cover in place. Start at the center of the listing and work from side to side until you complete the horseshoe.

Next, carefully roll the two top corners into position and pull the cover completely over the frame; then very carefully pull the cover down and roll the two lower corners over (Fig. 1-39). Turn the front backrest over so it is face down. Starting at the bottom center, hog-ring the flap only. Next, go to the top of the cover and, starting at the center top, hog-ring the cover in place. As you work around the top corners pull the cover downward to eliminate wrinkles in the side facing.

After the cover is completely hog-ringed, locate the hole next to the outside arm that holds the ½ inch chrome bolt and chrome washer and

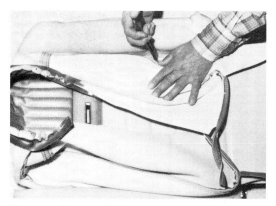

Fig. 1-38. Fasten side listings on Pony front back-rest before rolling top corners into position.

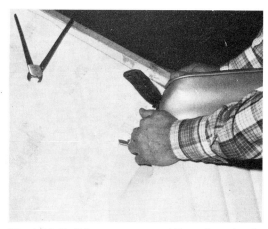

Fig. 1-39. Roll lower corners of Pony front back-rest into position and hog-ring.

Fig. 1-40. New cardboard panels have extra clip holes to fit several different year models. Lay old cover on top of new one to locate proper holes for clips.

Fig. 1-41. Next, install new panel.

lock nut. Cut the material away from the hole, screw the nut halfway onto the bolt, place the chrome washer onto the bolt and install the bolt. Do not tighten completely, as you will want to adjust the angle of the backrest to suit you after the seat is installed in the car.

Remove the clips (Fig. 1-40) from the old panel board that fits on the back of the frontrest. Notice the position they were facing, then install them in the new panel board in the same position (Fig. 1-41). Count the number of clips in the backboard and locate the corresponding round holes on the back of the seat frame. Cut the material away from the holes and snap the cover in place (Fig. 1-42).

Step 5: Installing

If you are going to replace the headlining, carpeting or dashboard, do not install the seats until these items are completed. However, if you are not replacing these items, you are now ready to attach the front backrest to the front cushion and install the seats in the car.

Starting with the shorter arm, which is the inside arm, place the protective washer on the pin, then slide the shorter arm over the pin.

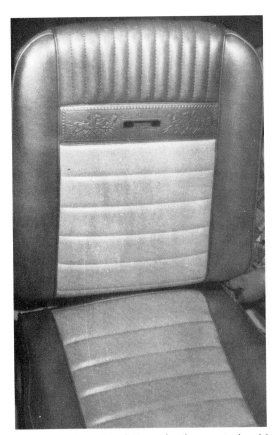

Fig. 1-42. Completed Pony bucket seat should look like this.

Fig. 1-43. Before shot of a pair of 1965 front buckets.

Fig. 1-44. After complete restoration the same 1965 front buckets look quite different!

Next, place the protective washer on the opposite pin and, using a very heavy piece of cardboard to protect the cover, pry the outside arm over the pin. Insert the two hairpin clips into the pins so that neither arm can come off.

Place the plastic cover over the inside arm and screw in place. Then put the chrome outside arm cover in place and make sure to use the plastic spacers so as not to bend the chrome trim, and screw in place. Double check to make sure you have used the blunt-end Phillips screw at the lower end of the arm; otherwise, when the front backrest is moved forward, it will cut the side facing (Fig. 1-43, 1-44).

To install the seats in the car, just reverse the procedure you used to remove them. Start with the rear backrest. Hang it in place and install the two 7/16 bolts in the slots at the bottom of the backrest. Lift the seat belts and slide the rear cushion in place and snap it down on the safety locks.

Place the bucket seats in position and drop the seat bolts over the corresponding holes in the floor. Go under the car and install the ½ nuts and washers from the underside of the car. Replace the rubber grommets in their proper positions.

Chapter 2

Door and quarter panels, and padded dash

Replacing the standard door panels or padded dash on a Mustang is relatively simple. There are two basic steps: removing and installing.

The front and rear Pony panels and convertible rear quarter panels are a little more involved. There are four basic steps: removing, stripping, replacing and installing.

Here is a list of tools and supplies you will need for either type.

Phillips screwdriver	Scratch awl
Straight screwdriver	Electric drill
Socket set	1/8 inch drill bit
Diagonal side cutters	1/8 inch aluminum pop rivets
Window regulator and door handle clip remover (1965 only), tool no. 21812-B	Allen wrench set
	Putty knife
Pop rivet gun	Needle-nose pliers
Rubber mallet	Spray glue/contact trim cement

Step 1: Removing
Standard door panels

Starting with the front doors on 1964½ and early 1965 models only, use tool no. 21812-B to remove the window regulator handle and the door handle (Fig. 2-1). Remember the position of the door handle

Fig. 2-1. When removing the 1964½ and 1965 door handles, insert tool in opposite direction of handle.

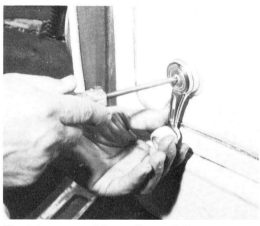

Fig. 2-2. 1967 and later all use Phillips screws to hold inside door and window handles.

before you remove it so you will be able to replace it correctly. The 1966 models use an Allen bolt to hold the handles in place. The 1967-70 models use Phillips screws (Fig. 2-2). Keep the large plastic washers with the handles; they keep the handle from cutting the material on the door panels (Fig. 2-3).

Remove the two Phillips screws under the armrest on 1965 and 1966 models, and remove the armrest and base as a unit. Slide a putty knife between the door panel and metal inner door until you come to each door panel clip. Pry outward and pop the clip out of each hole (Fig. 2-4). Remove the door panel and the springs on the window regulator and door handle shafts. Be sure to replace them — they hold tension on the door and window handles to prevent rattles and keep the panel tight against the handles.

Lay the new panel face down on a clean table and place the old panel above it (Fig. 2-5). Visually check all the clips in the old panel.

Fig. 2-3. Always re-use plastic spacer between door handle and panel to prevent damage to door panel.

Fig. 2-4. Slide putty knife along outer edge to locate door clips and pop out.

Fig. 2-5. Reproduction door panels are available through Mustang specialty shops (Jeff Tann/Argus Publishers Corporation)

Replace any bent, broken or missing clips with new ones (part no. 205, with rubber insert). Remove the usable clips from the old door panel, one at a time, and place them in the same position into the new door panel.

Padded dash

The padded dashes on the 1965 and 1966 Mustangs look similar at first glance, but there are some differences in appearance and installation. They are interchangeable, but the real purist or restorer would know the difference, so it is advisable to replace your padded dash with the proper one. The 1967 and 1968 Mustang padded dashes are identical in appearance and installation. The only difference between the 1969 and 1970 pads shows up depending on whether the car has air conditioning or not.

1965 and 1966

Remove the Phillips screws in the moldings at the front edge of the dash (Fig. 2-6). The Phillips screws at the ends are longer; as you remove them, put them in order on a piece of masking tape, so you can replace them properly.

Remove the speaker and defroster grilles. Remove the speaker and check it to see if it should be replaced. Remove the two clips on either side of the defroster outlets with needle-nose pliers, and remove the defroster outlets and hoses. Reach in through the speaker hole and remove the two 3/8 inch nuts holding the center section of the dash in place.

1965 only

There are two chrome moldings under the padded dash (Fig. 2-7). One starts at the driver's door post (Fig. 2-8) where the padded dash

Fig. 2-6. Removing the molding at the front edge of the padded dash is much easier with a long Phillips screwdriver.

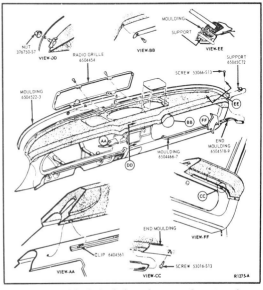

Fig. 2-7. Padded dash breakaway drawing from the 1965 Ford Mustang factory manual.

meets the metal portion of the dash and has two Phillips screws in the curved end at the door post. There is one screw in the straight end over the instrument cluster (Fig. 2-9).

The opposite side molding starts at the passenger's door post (Fig. 2-10) and has two screws in the curved end at the door post and one screw in the straight end over the glovebox door (Fig. 2-11).

Remove the three Phillips screws, two on one end and one on the other end of each molding. Then, using a thin straight screwdriver, go between the molding and the dash, locate the two spring clips and pop the molding off. Reach in around the speaker opening and lift the dash slightly, then pull the dash toward the rear of the car to free any glued areas. After the dash is removed, clean the glue from the upper metal ledge. If you are going to repaint the metal portion of the dash you should do it before installing the dash pad.

1966 only

The removal of the 1966 padded dash differs from the 1965 in the following ways:

The 1966 padded dash does not have the chrome molding over the instrument cluster and glovebox. Instead, it has four Phillips screws

Fig. 2-8. Curved trim at door post on driver's side.

Fig. 2-9. Right side of trim over temperature gauge.

Fig. 2-10. Curved trim at door post, passenger side.

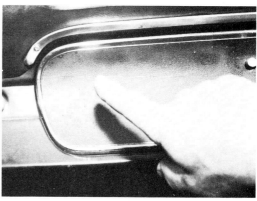

Fig. 2-11. Chrome trim over glovebox on 1964½ and 1965 Mustang.

that go into the padded portion of the dash over the instrument cluster, four Phillips screws over the glovebox door and two 3/8 nuts on each end of the dash.

1967 and 1968

The 1967 and 1968 padded dashes are identical except for the lower pad at the bottom edge of the instrument panel. Remove the Phillips screws holding the moldings at the front edge of the dash. Remove the four Phillips screws on the heater control assembly and pull the assembly out of the way (Fig. 2-12). Reach in the heater control opening and remove the nut holding the lower left end of the panel in place. Remove the three Phillips retaining screws holding the ashtray assembly in place and disconnect the hot lead from the back of the lighter.

Remove the five Phillips screws holding the instrument cluster in place. Reach in through the ashtray assembly opening and remove the nut holding the end of the instrument panel in place. Pull the instrument panel out slightly (Fig. 2-13). Open the glovebox door and reach in and remove the three retaining screws. Remove the retaining nuts from the lower center and upper finish panels and remove the panels. Remove the four screws from the front edge of the padded dash and pull the padded dash out.

1969 and 1970

There are end moldings on each side of the padded dash (Fig. 2-14). Remove the two screws in each end molding, remove the moldings and then the screws, one at each end of the dash (lower corners). Remove the three screws on the upper dash, one on each side of the defroster outlets and one in the center of the defroster outlets. Remove the two screws in the lower center of the pad and take out the dash. If your car is the Grande model you will have to disconnect the wires behind the clock before removing the dash.

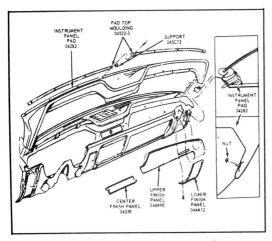

Fig. 2-12. Padded dash breakaway illustration from the 1967 Ford Mustang factory manual.

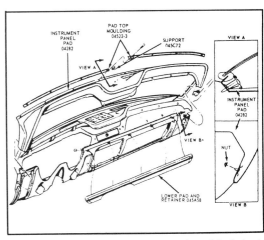

Fig. 2-13. Breakaway drawing of padded dash from the 1968 Ford Mustang factory manual.

Step 2: Installing
Standard door panel

If you are going to paint the interior of your car, this should be done prior to installing the door panel. Once you have either painted or cleaned the interior metal of the door, the installation is as follows. Check the water shield for tears (Fig. 2-15) and replace if necessary. (The water shield is the paper covering between the door panel and the metal frame of the door. It prevents water or moisture from reaching the backside of the door panel, causing the panel to warp.)

This is the ideal time to check the lower inside area of the door for leaves, debris and anything that may have been left there. Also, check the rollers in the window-raising mechanism for replacement if necessary. Be sure to grease the rollers and tracks and clean the drain holes at the lower portion of the doors (this prevents water from building up and causing the bottom of the door to rust). Check the large rubber stop that prevents the window from going down too far and make sure it is in place. Check all the bolts around the window regulator mechanism and the door-latching mechanism, and tighten as needed. You can also lubricate the door latch and locking mechanisms. (This is another example of how you can do a more thorough and better job than most professionals.)

Starting at the lower front edge of the door, insert the two pointed edges of the clip into the hole and press it until the clip locks in place. Continue in sequence and finish the lower edge of the door. Next, while the upper half is still loose, place the two springs over the door handle and window regulator shafts. Press into place the center forward clip and the upper front clip. Finish off the top row of clips and go around the curve at the rear portion of the door panel (Fig. 2-16).

Put the large plastic washers onto the door and window handles and fasten into place. Cut a tiny hole for the armrest base and put back

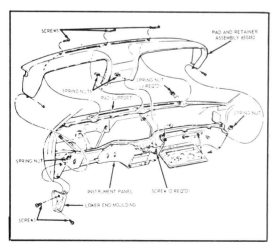

Fig. 2-14. Padded dash breakaway drawing from the 1969-70 Ford Mustang factory manual.

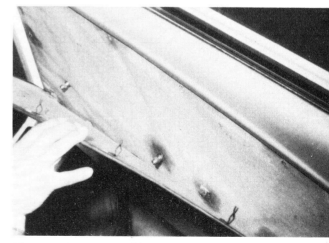

Fig. 2-15. Note material between door panel and door.

the two Phillips screws that hold the armrest (Fig. 2-17). This procedure is for all standard front door panels from 1965 through 1970 including coupes, convertibles and fastbacks.

Padded dash

1965 and 1966

As previously stated, you should disconnect the battery when working around the electrical area of the car or when leaving the doors open for prolonged periods.

Apply contact cement on the two metal mounting surfaces on the dash. Then apply contact cement on the corresponding area of the padded dash. Allow to dry several minutes. Line up the two holes in the dash with the two bolts in the padded dash. Push the two bolts into place and press both ends of the dashboard into position until the speaker opening is in place. On the 1966, also line up the two outer bolts on each end. Reach in through the speaker opening and tighten the two nuts. Push the defroster outlets into place and replace the two clips on either side, making sure they catch the holes in the dash panel. Replace the speaker and the two screws holding the speaker grille in place. Replace the upper dash molding, making sure you use the long Phillips screws at the ends and the shorter ones along the front.

1965 only

Using a scratch awl, locate the inside Phillips screw on the lower edge of the padded dash. Put the screw in partway and locate the two holes for the clips. Press the clips into place. This leaves the short curved piece to install. Slide the curved piece into the long straight piece. Use a scratch awl to locate the holes and put in the other two Phillips screws. Tighten all three screws and use a single-edge blade or an X-Acto knife to cut any excess vinyl from the lower edge of the chrome trim.

Fig. 2-16. Line up clips and press into place.

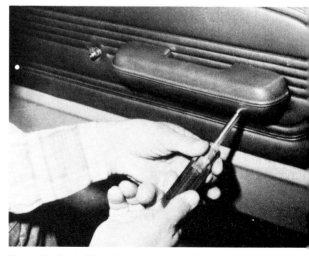

Fig. 2-17. Installing the armrest on the 1967 door panel.

1966 only

Use a scratch awl to locate the four holes over the instrument cluster and the four holes over the glovebox door, and install the eight screws.

1967 and 1968

Place the padded dash in position by lining up the two studs on either end with the holes in the metal portion of the dash. When these studs are in place, push the upper portion of the dash forward against the windshield, line up the four holes at the forward edge of the dash and install the four screws. On the left side, reach in through the heater assembly opening and install the retaining nuts on the lower end of the padded dash. Next, go to the right side and install the lower retaining nut.

Place the center and upper finish panels in place and install the retainer screws. Place the lower right finish panel against the instrument panel and install the retaining nut and screws. Move the instrument cluster into position and install the Phillips screws. Connect the hot lead on the lighter, place the ashtray assembly into position and replace the three Phillips screws. Place the heater control assembly into position and install the four Phillips screws. Place the glovebox assembly into position and install the three retaining screws. Place the moldings at the front edge of the dash into position and use a scratch awl to locate the holes. (Just as in the 1965 and 1966 models, the longer screws are on the outside edges and the shorter ones along the front.)

1969 and 1970

Check to make sure all the spring nuts are properly located. Connect the clock wires and position the dash pad in place. Install the two screws holding the lower center pad to the instrument panel. Use a scratch awl to line up the three upper dash pad screws on the front of

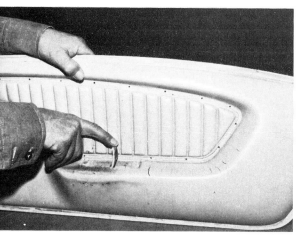

Fig. 2-18. Remove plate in Pony door panel to expose the two Phillips screws holding panel to door.

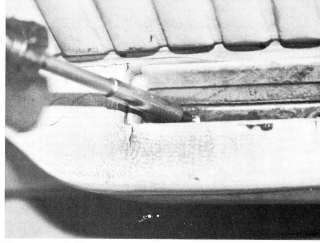

Fig. 2-19. Phillips screws must be removed before door panel is removed.

the dash, and install them. Install the two screws, one on each end of the dash pad, and tighten all screws. Install the two screws in each end molding and the installation is complete.

Step 1:   Removing
Pony front door panel
The Pony door panel has a built-in armrest. In the recessed portion of the armrest is a covered metal plate (Fig. 2-18). Remove this plate with a straight screwdriver, exposing two Phillips screws. Remove the two screws (Fig. 2-19). In the chrome trim around the outer edge of the door panel you will find another Phillips screw; remove it. Remove the door handle and window regulator handle (use the same procedure as on the regular panel, even though the handles are shaped differently). Insert a putty knife between the chrome trim around the door panel and the inner door sheet metal, and pry the clips out. Once the door panel is removed, use the same procedure as on the standard door panel (check the water shield and clean or paint as necessary).
Pony rear quarter panel
Remove the rear seat and rear backrest as described earlier. The Pony rear quarter panel has a chrome cap at the upper front edge of the panel. Remove the Phillips screw and the chrome cap and pull off the snap-on windlace (Fig. 2-20). Remove the door sill molding and the window regulator handle. Remove the Phillips screws and take out the rear quarter panel.
Convertible rear quarter panel
Remove the rear seat and rear backrest. Remove the rear window regulator handle (Fig. 2-21) and pull the snap-on windlace away from the front edge of the panel. Note the little opening at the upper edge of the metal portion of the panel and remember how the snap-on windlace fits under the opening to cover the raw edge. (This is the same as the regular quarter panel.)

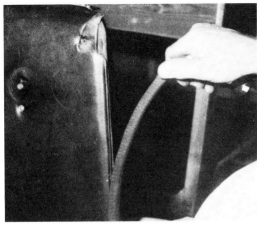

Fig. 2-20. Remove snap-on windlace before removing Pony rear quarter panel.

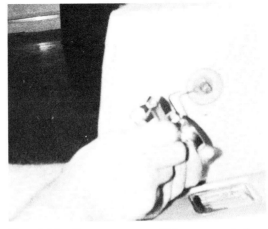

Fig. 2-21. Remove convertible rear window handle with Allen wrench.

Remove the door sill molding and take out the seven Phillips screws holding the panel in place. There are three Phillips screws at the rear of the panel concealed under the cushion and backrest. There are two at the front edge of the panel in the upholstery. There is one Phillips screw below the handle and one Phillips screw at the top rear section. The convertible top has to be lowered halfway to expose the last screw (Fig. 2-22). After you remove these screws, pull the lower section of the panel out to clear the window regulator and lift the panel up and out.

Step 2: Stripping
Pony front door panel

If you are going to install new Pony door panels, use this procedure: Place the door panel face down on a table and remove the tiny Phillips screws that hold the back of the chrome in place on the door panel. These are located at the front edge of the outer chrome and are usually covered with tiny strips of tape. Starting at the upper front corner of the door panel, pull the chrome molding away from the edge of the panel and carefully work your way across the top edge, around the curve and across the lower edge (Fig. 2-23). Be careful not to bend the chrome while removing it. The inner chrome molding is held in place with bent-over metal tabs. Straighten the tabs and pull the molding off (Fig. 2-24).

Fig. 2-22. Lower convertible top part way to expose Phillips screw at rear of convertible quarter panel.

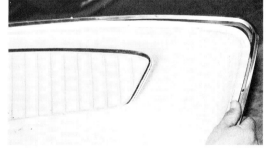

Fig. 2-23. Remove outer chrome trim around Pony door panel.

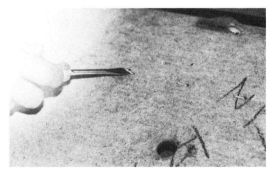

Fig. 2-24. Carefully straighten metal tabs holding inner chrome trim on Pony door panel.

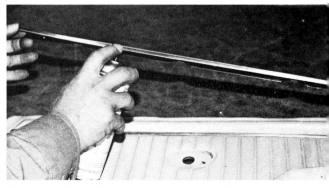

Fig. 2-25. Use silicon spray in groove before installing chrome on edge of Pony door panel.

Now is a good time to clean the chrome while it is off the panel. After the chrome is cleaned, spray a light coat of silicon into the groove of the outer chrome molding so the panel will go in easily (Fig. 2-25).

Pony rear quarter panel

Lay the rear quarter panel face down on the table. The window felt at the front upper half of the panel must be removed. Cut the staples with your diagonal side cutters, and pull the felt away from the panel (Fig. 2-26). If the felt is still good, clean the chrome bead and replace the felt after the panel is covered. Next, pull the glued edge of the material away from the backside of the panel (Fig. 2-27).

The sewn replacement cover for the rear quarter panel has a single seam sewn into it just like the original. Some early models had no seam. (If yours did not, check the photo to locate the position of the seam.) There are cutouts in the metal at the upper and lower edges of the panel (Fig. 2-28).

Be sure to check the position of the seam before removing the cover. A helpful hint would be to remove one cover and leave the other cover in place to check the correct position of the seam.

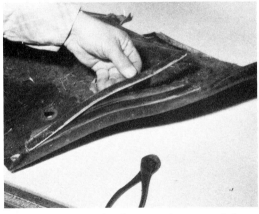

Fig. 2-26. Cut staples loose and remove felt on Pony quarter panels before re-covering.

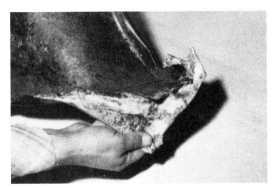

Fig. 2-27. Pull glued old material away from panel and remove cover.

Fig. 2-28. Cutouts help in the positioning process.

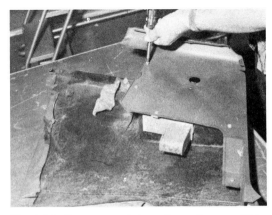

Fig. 2-29. Remove metal portion of convertible quarter panel from upholstered section.

Convertible rear quarter panel

Remove the five Phillips screws holding the metal section to the covered section of the panel (Fig. 2-29). This is the ideal time to clean and repaint the metal panel (Fig. 2-30). You can mask the chrome and felt, or remove it. The felt is held in place by wire staples. Cut the staples loose and remove the felt. If the upper snap in the metal is good, you can mask it off; if not, drill it out on the back side using a 1/8 inch drill bit.

Slide the ashtray cover back and pull out the center section of the ashtray. Bend the four tabs inward and pull out the ashtray chrome trim and slide the top together (Fig. 2-31). This is the ideal time to clean and lubricate the ashtray and sliding top. Also clean and paint the ashtray receptacle.

Drill out the three snaps on the upper portion of the upholstered panel and remove the covering. Again, leave one panel covered so you can refer to it while you are re-covering the other panel.

Step 3: Replacing
Pony front door panel

Originally, I planned to explain how to re-cover the Pony front door panels with a door skin. Upon considering the procedure, I have decided not to go into this detail for several reasons: The procedure is difficult and time consuming, and there are now reasonably priced reproduction panels. The cost of the skins alone is nearly as expensive as complete panels.

You will need to replace the trim after you have installed a panel. Use a scratch awl to punch holes in the new Pony door panel for the inner chrome trim (Fig. 2-32). Install the inner chrome molding first; be

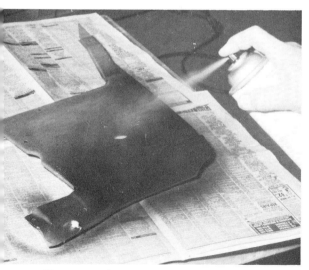

Fig. 2-30. Clean and spray paint panel before assembly.

Fig. 2-31. Ashtray holder must be removed from rear quarter panel.

careful not to break the prongs. Place the outer chrome trim behind the door panel and, starting at the upper front edge, press the chrome over the edge of the panel (Fig. 2-33). Work your way across the top edge, around the curve and across the lower edge. Replace the tiny Phillips screws that keep the molding in place. Replace any broken, missing or bent clips (Fig. 2-34).

Pony rear quarter panel

After you remove the replacement Pony rear quarter panel covers from the kit box and check to see that you have a left and right side, allow the covers to sit in the sun or at room temperature to make the Naugahyde softer and more pliable.

Lay the metal panel face up and place the material in position. Make sure you have enough material to wrap around all the edges (Fig. 2-35). Turn the panel over with the material in place and apply glue to the edge of the metal and the edge of the material. Allow the glue to dry—contact cement will hold only when the glue is dry to the touch.

Starting at the upper rear section of the panel, glue the seam first and then glue about two inches on either side of the seam. Pull tightly on the opposite end of the seam and press into place, also the two inches

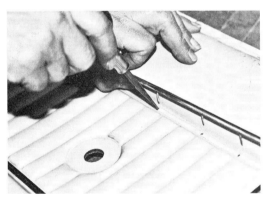

Fig. 2-32. Place inner chrome on panel and pre-punch holes for tabs before installing.

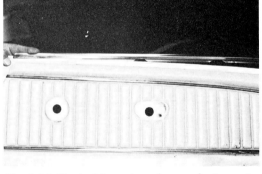

Fig. 2-33. Start at top edge when replacing outer chrome trim on Pony door panel.

Fig. 2-34. Use old panel to help line up door clips properly.

Fig. 2-35. Use a clamp to hold seam in place and check cover before gluing.

on either side of the seam. Pull the material gently forward and glue the entire front edge of the panel. Pull the material over the top edge and smooth out any wrinkles. Pull the material gently down and glue the bottom edge, again working out wrinkles.

Pull the material over the rear top curved section and glue in place (Fig. 2-36). Pull the bottom down, glue into place and smooth out any wrinkles. Finally, glue the last section in place and your rear quarter panel is covered.

If your window felt was good, you can clean it and install it as follows. Position the felt in place and drill a 1/8 inch hole at the front edge. Use a 1/8 inch aluminum pop rivet to fasten the front. Keep the top edge of the chrome on the felt even with the top of the panel. Drill holes approximately every two inches and pop rivet into place.

Before you remove the cover from the opposite panel, check to see which holes are used and punch new holes in the newly covered panel with a scratch awl.

Fig. 2-36. Stretch material over corner and glue, making sure wrinkles are all smooth in exposed areas.

Fig. 2-37. Check rear quarter upholstery pieces to make sure they are correct.

Fig. 2-38. Start convertible rear quarter installation at seam where armrest meets upright.

Fig. 2-39. When glue is dry on both surfaces, press material in place.

Convertible rear quarter panel

After you have purchased your convertible rear quarter trim kit, remove it from the package and lay it out in the sun or at room temperature to remove wrinkles and soften the vinyl. Also check to be sure you have a left and a right side (Fig. 2-37).

Position the cover in place, making sure the front corner seam and the seam behind the ashtray are properly located (Fig. 2-38). Turn the panel over, face down, and glue the seam at the front and rear edges. Glue the seam behind the ashtray. Do not pull this section too tight as it will cause the main seam to look crooked. Glue the section from the front seam back, then glue the entire panel except the upper portion (Fig. 2-39). Make slits in the material to go around inside corners (Fig. 2-40), and darts to go around outside corners.

Glue the top and bottom of the ledge on the upper portion of the panel (Fig. 2-41), then work the material in place until all the wrinkles are out. Glue the bottom edge of the ledge in place. This area will show, and care should be taken with it. When you are through covering the panel, locate the three snap holes and pop rivet the new snaps into place. You can also use a machine thread snap with a washer and nut (Fig. 2-42).

If your window felt is good, you can clean and replace it. Position the felt in place and drill a 1/8 inch hole at the front edge. Use a 1/8 inch aluminum pop rivet to fasten the front. Keeping the top edge even, drill holes approximately every two inches and pop rivet into place.

Locate the opening for the ashtray and cut an X in the material from corner to corner (Fig. 2-43). Lower the ashtray receptacle into place and bend the tabs outward. Check the sliding cover and drop the ashtray receptacle into place. Screw the metal section back onto the

Fig. 2-40. *Always cut slits on backside of upholstery when going around inside curves.*

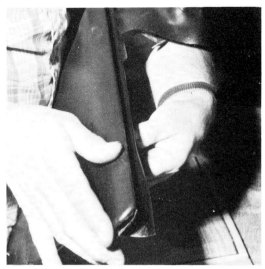

Fig. 2-41. *Pull material over top edge of convertible rear quarter panel and glue on ledge.*

covered section. From the backside, use a scratch awl to punch out the three holes at the rear of the panel and the two at the front. Your panel is now ready to be installed, and you are ready to strip and re-cover the other side.

Step 4: Installing
Pony front door panel
Install the door panel as previously outlined for standard panels.

Pony rear quarter panel
When you have completed both panels, install them in the car following the removal instructions in reverse order.

The 1965-66 Pony door panels and the 1967 and 1968 deluxe door panels are being reproduced by several manufacturers. The 1969 and 1970 deluxe door panels have been developed by major manufacturers and are available through specialty shops. However, all Pony and deluxe panels will be minus the stainless or chrome trim. You will have to save and reuse your trim or find suitable used trim components. The procedures are the same for these panels.

Convertible rear quarter panel
Be sure all the insulation is in place on all the quarter panels before installing (Fig. 2-44).

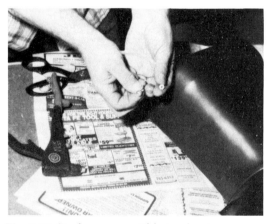

Fig. 2-42. Replace convertible top boot snaps on quarter panels with snaps and nuts or pop rivets.

Fig. 2-43. Cut from corner to corner forming an X before replacing the ashtray holder.

Fig. 2-44. Comparing the old convertible quarter panel with the new one.

Chapter 3

Headliner

The headliner is probably the most mysterious part of the interior. Though people see it in place, very few of them know or understand what is holding it there. By following these step-by-step instructions you can install your own headliner with professional-looking results.

There are two ways to install the headliner — the right way and the wrong way. We will concern ourselves with the right way only, which includes removing the windshield and rear window on most models.

Here is a list of tools and supplies you will need.

Shears
No. 2 or medium-size Phillips screwdriver
2 medium-size straight screwdrivers
Chrome removal tool, part no. T64P-42430-R or -L
Headliner glue kit
Rubber mallet
8 feet of 1/8 inch sash cord
Windshield sealant
Silicon spray
Set of Allen wrenches
Electrical tape, 1967-68 only
2 inch dull putty knife

There are three basic steps to properly installing a headliner: inspecting and planning, removing, and replacing.

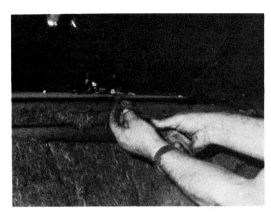

Fig. 3-1. Remove the two clips holding the package tray.

Fig. 3-2. Remove the panel board strips holding rear lower section of the headlining in place.

Step 1: Inspecting and planning

Now is the ideal time to check the rubber around the windshield and rear window, the snap-on windlace, the sun visors and the package tray. Once you have decided what you need to replace, you can order everything at the same time. (For example, it would be foolish to install the headliner, only to find at a later date you needed to replace the rubber seal around one of the windows.) All the items you will need are available at your Mustang specialty shop.

Step 2: Removing

Remove the rear cushion and rear backrest as outlined earlier. On the coupe model, remove the two metal clips holding the package tray in place (Fig. 3-1) and then take out the package tray. Under the package tray, on either side, you will notice two strips of hard panel board holding the headliner in place with two bent-over metal prongs

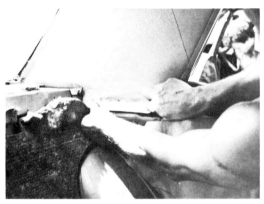

Fig. 3-3. Pull headlining down and lift away from prongs. Note this area is not glued because it covers the bolt holding the outside chrome molding for the landau top.

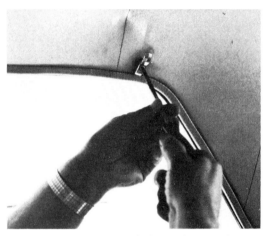

Fig. 3-4. Remove screw holding the coat hanger and replace screw for later location.

Fig. 3-5. Replace all three screws for sun visor location.

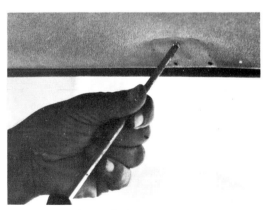

Fig. 3-6. Replace all three screws for rearview mirror location.

(Fig. 3-2). Gently lift the metal clips and remove the two pieces of panel board. In front of the package tray on either side you will notice short V-shaped prongs holding the headliner in place. (This area is not glued, so you can remove the landau top molding when replacing a landau top on models so equipped.) Pull downward on the headliner to free it from the V-shaped prongs (Fig. 3-3). Remove the coat hangers on either side above the quarter windows, and put the screws back into the holes (Fig. 3-4). Remove the sun visors and put the screws back into the holes (Fig. 3-5). Remove the rearview mirror and put the screws back into the holes (Fig. 3-6). If your coupe is a 1967 or 1968 model, remove the lens and the dome light, take out the screws, unplug the wires, cover the wires with electrical tape and put the screws back in place (Fig. 3-7). On the 1965-66 models, remove the two metal ends at the upper portion of the windshield post. On the 1967-68 models, use a straight screwdriver to remove the upholstered windshield posts, which are held in place with three door-panel-style clips (Fig. 3-8). Next, remove the snap-on trim by pulling it away from the metal lip (Fig. 3-9).

Fig. 3-7. For 1967 and later models, remove dome light and replace screws.

Fig. 3-8. Use a screwdriver to remove 1967 and later padded windshield posts.

Fig. 3-9. Snap-on trim easily pulls away from edge of headlining.

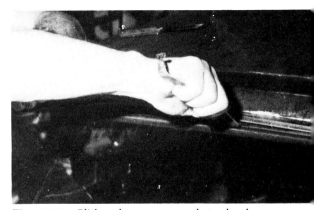

Fig. 3-10. Slide chrome-removal tool along chrome to locate clips.

Going to the outside of the car, on the 1965-66 models, remove the rear molding with the chrome removal tool (Fig. 3-10). Remove the front molding in the same way (Fig. 3-11). On the 1967-68 models the upper stainless molding and the side moldings around the rear window are held in place with Phillips screws (Fig. 3-12); the lower molding is the same as on the 1965-66.

Place blankets on the trunk and hood. Go back to the inside of the car and remove the rear window by working the rubber over the lip with the two straight screwdrivers. Next, remove the windshield in the same manner, being careful not to crack it. (Some people may choose to have a glass shop remove and replace the windshield, rather than risk breaking the glass; but if you are careful and follow the instructions you should be able to do the windows yourself with minimal risk.) If you have decided to replace the rubber you can cut it loose with a razor knife and reduce the risk of breaking the glass.

Pull the old headliner loose from the lip at the windshield, the lip at the rear window and along both sides above the door windows and both quarter windows (Fig. 3-13). Starting at the front of the car, push the

Fig. 3-11. Use a putty knife to lift chrome away while sliding tool to remove chrome from clips.

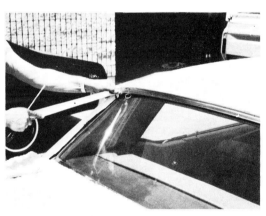

Fig. 3-12. Rear chrome on 1967 and later is held in place with Phillips screws.

Fig. 3-13. After removing window, pull glued edge away from opening.

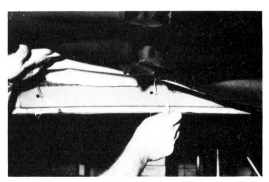

Fig. 3-14. Note two sets of holes for bows. Mark set used before removing old headlining.

bows to the rear. After marking the bow holes used, take each bow loose from the sides (Fig. 3-14). When you reach the last bow you will notice two steel wires holding it in position. Push the last bow to the rear of the car and leave the wires in place, attached to the lip around the rear window (Fig. 3-15). Before removing the bows from the headliner, use pieces of masking tape and number the bows from one to four starting at the front. (All coupes from 1965 to 1970 have four bows.) Remove the bows from the headliner and clean as necessary. If they have some rust on them you might want to clean them with steel wool and repaint them.

If your car is a fastback the procedure around the windshield is the same; however, you will have to remove the molding and interior trim held in place with Phillips screws. You will notice that the factory installed the headliner before installing the rear window. If you are doing a complete restoration and removing the rear window, I would advise you to install the headliner in the same sequence. If not, it is not necessary to remove the rear window, on the fastback only. You will also notice the 1965-68 fastbacks have three bows, the 1969-70 fastbacks have four bows and they all have steel wires to hold the rear bow in place.

Step 3: Replacing

Before installing the new headliner, check the roof insulation and reglue it where needed. Do not install the headliner without gluing the insulation back in place; otherwise, the headliner will not be smooth and tight. Insert the bows into the listing, starting with the number 1 bow (Fig. 3-16). When all the bows are in place, check to make sure they are exactly centered. Take the headliner and, starting with the rear bow, insert the two ends into the holes previously marked and pull

Fig. 3-15. Note the two wire clips holding the last bow in place to keep headlining from coming too far forward.

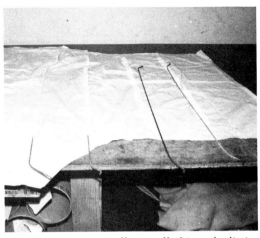

Fig. 3-16. Bows partially installed into the listing of the headlining on the 1965-70 models will look like this.

forward until the two steel wires lock the rear bow in place and keep it from moving forward (Fig. 3-17).

Working from the rear forward, put the remaining bows in place and continue pulling forward on the headliner. Now that the headliner is hung, check from side to side to make sure it is still centered.

Apply glue to the inside front lip at the windshield, pull the headliner forward gently and touch it up against the lip to transfer the glue line to the headliner. Once this is done, pull the headliner away and reglue the inside metal lip. Also, apply more glue to the glue line on the backside of the headliner. Allow the glue to dry completely to the touch — the time will vary according to temperature and weather conditions.

When the glue is completely dry (does not stick to your finger), pull the headliner forward and attach at the center first, right below the rearview mirror. Next, while holding this in place with one hand, pull forward and outward and touch the area right below the sun visor. Repeat on the opposite side. Then, gently pulling forward, press together along the entire front of the headliner (Fig. 3-18). While doing

Fig. 3-17. Start installation by centering the headlining and catching the last bow on the retaining clips.

Fig. 3-18. After the front center is glued in place, pull forward and out to each side and glue.

Fig. 3-19. Slide hand along seam to smooth out wrinkles from side to side before gluing.

Fig. 3-20. Be careful to spray glue only on the metal lip.

this, look at the seam in the number 1 bow and keep it as straight as possible (Fig. 3-19).

Next, glue the entire inside lip around the rear window opening and repeat the procedure used on the windshield (Fig. 3-20). Once you have the windshield and rear window glued into place, make several cuts to relieve the tension on the arc over the rear quarter windows (Fig. 3-21). Glue the lip on either side (Fig. 3-22), approximately 3/8 inch wide. Press the headliner against the glue then reglue each side and the glue line on the back of the headliner. Allow to dry, then press in place.

Pull the headliner into position and replace the two cardboard strips holding the headliner in place under the package tray (Fig. 3-23). Make your cut at the front edge of the package tray and catch the remainder onto the metal prongs (Fig. 3-24).

From the outside of the car, trim the headliner about ½ inch away from the metal lip around the windshield, rear window and both sides over the door windows and quarter windows (Fig. 3-25). Glue the metal lip and the remaining ½ inch of the headliner and allow to dry. Make several slits at the corners and curves, then fold over and glue in place (Fig. 3-26).

Fig. 3-21. Make slits on each side of the seams before gluing. Be careful to keep slits at least one-half inch away from metal lip.

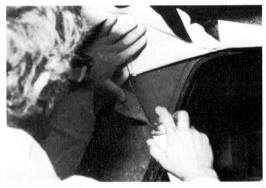

Fig. 3-22. Make sure padding in rear quarter of headlining is in place before gluing headlining.

Fig. 3-23. Replace cardboard strips to hold headlining in place and bend tabs.

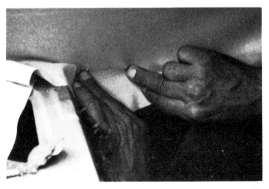

Fig. 3-24. Pull headlining material down to catch on V-shaped prongs.

If you are going to replace the rubber, remove the old rubber from the glass, put the new rubber in place and use windshield sealant (Fig. 3-27). After the rubber is in place around the glass, place the cord in the groove that fits over the metal lip, go completely around the glass and criss-cross the cord at the center bottom edge (Fig. 3-28). Position the rear window in place and slowly pull the cord over the metal lip until the rear window is in place (Fig. 3-29). Repeat on the windshield.

If your car has a vinyl top and you are going to replace it, do not put the stainless moldings in place yet. If your car does not have a vinyl top, seal the rubber around the lip with sealant and install the stainless molding immediately.

Locate and cut a tiny hole around each screw holding the rearview mirror, sun visors and coat hangers (Fig. 3-30). If your car is a 1967-68 you will also have to remove the screws that hold the dome light in place and make a cut for the wires to come through. If your car is a 1965-66 you will have two metal ends at the upper windshield post (Fig.

Fig. 3-25. Cut away excess material around window openings; leave one-half inch to glue and fold over.

Fig. 3-26. Cut slits around inside curves before gluing.

Fig. 3-27. Start at a corner and place the rubber around the glass.

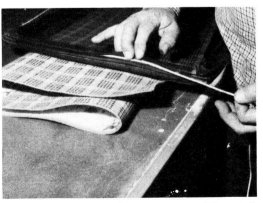

Fig. 3-28. Start at the bottom center of the windshield or rear window and put the cord in the groove that fits over the metal lip opening.

3-31). The 1967-68 model cars have the removable upholstered windshield posts.

Measure your snap-on trim and, starting at the rear quarter window, use a rubber mallet to tap the snap-on into place. Clean and install the rearview mirror bracket, the sun visor brackets and coat hangers. Install the sun visors onto the brackets. On the 1965-66 models, clean or paint, if necessary, the two metal ends at the upper windshield post. On the 1967-68 models, snap the windshield post in place. Install the package tray and clean and replace the dome light (install a new bulb if needed). Your headliner is now complete.

Some of these steps are shortcut by some shops — such as removing the windows, painting the bows and regluing the insulation. This is another example of how your job can be as good as, or better than, that of some shops.

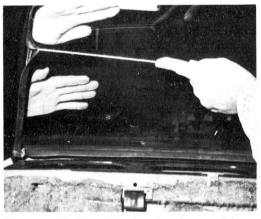

Fig. 3-29. Position the glass in place and have someone hold the glass on the outside while you pull the cord and pull the rubber over the lip. Always start at the bottom center and work both sides to the top center.

Fig. 3-30. Cut an opening between the sun visor screws and cut tiny holes for the sun visor screws.

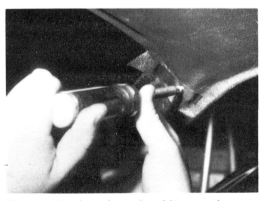

Fig. 3-31. Replace the end moldings on the 1965 and 1966 windshield posts.

Chapter 4

Landau top

Replacing the landau top is not a difficult task. You can do it for about one-third the cost of having it done in a shop, and by following the instructions your job will be just as professional looking.

Here is a list of tools and supplies you will need.

Dull putty knife
Phillips screwdriver
Set of Allen wrenches
3/8 inch deep-well socket with short extension
Tool no. T64P-42430-R or -L (chrome removal tool)
6 foot straightedge, flexible
No. 2 lead pencil
2 single-edge razor blades
1 ½ inch masking tape
4 cans contact spray glue
1 inch wooden paint mixer (sand to round corners)
Shears
Diagonal side cutters
Scratch awl

There are three basic steps to replacing a landau top: stripping the old top, preparing the car and installing the new top.

Step 1: Stripping the old top

In the previous chapter on headliners I covered removing the stainless around the windshield and rear window. If you replaced your headliner and you were also going to do a landau top I suggested you leave the stainless trim off until the landau top was complete.

Remove the rear seat, rear backrest and both rear quarter panels. When the quarter panels are removed you will see a section of headlining held in place by V-shaped prongs. Pull downward on the headliner to free it from the prongs, then raise the headliner enough to expose the two cutouts leading to the nuts holding the landau chrome trim in place. Using a 3/8 inch deep-well socket and a short extension remove the two speed nuts at the center and forward portion of the molding. Next, open the trunk and reach up at the roof beltline to remove the third speed nut at the end of the molding on both sides. It is a good idea to put a little Dum-Dum in the socket so that the speed nut will stick to the socket and not fall down in the inner fender panel where it would be impossible to recover. (Dum-Dum is a pliable, sticky material that is commonly used as a filler when body parts are bolted together under the floorboards and in panels, but it works great for this, too.) Remove the moldings and set them aside until you are ready to replace them.

Starting at the rear under the molding, pull the edges of the top away from the metal. Pull as much as possible off by hand and use a dull putty knife to scrape off whatever is left, being careful not to go through the paint and expose bare metal. Note that the original tops installed by the factory have a series of staples around the rear and front window openings. The factory also used a steel drive nail on most of the earlier models on the seams, front and rear.

Remove the drive nails very carefully by twisting them counterclockwise with a pair of diagonal side cutters. Be careful not to hit or touch the edge of the glass, as this will cause the windshield to crack or the rear window to shatter. Carefully pull the material free from the staples and leave the staples in place. Be sure to get all of the old material out of the rain gutter and drip rail. After the top is completely stripped, cut the staples with the diagonal side cutters and remove them.

Step 2: Preparing the car

Now that the old top is off the car, clean the glue off the metal using a lacquer thinner (be careful not to get lacquer thinner on the paint). After the top is completely cleaned, check to see if there is any rust. If there is, clean and sand the rust and prime the areas with a rust-inhibiting primer. After the top is cleaned and prepared, mask off the following: windshield, rear window, rear area ¼ inch above the landau chrome molding, and the drip rail from the lower end of the windshield post up and over the windows to the rear corner that meets the chrome molding (Fig. 4-1, 4-2). Locate the center of the top both at the windshield and at the rear window. Using a flexible straightedge, draw a pencil line from front to rear on the top of the roof (Fig. 4-3).

Fig. 4-1. Masking off the front of the car keeps glue off the windshield.

Fig. 4-2. Also mask off rear section of car.

Step 3: Installing the new top

Lay the new landau top face down on a table and find the center between the two seams at the rear and find the center between the two seams at the front. Using a straightedge, draw a pencil line from front to rear which will give you a center line on the bottom (wrong) side of the top. Caution: Always use a no. 2 soft lead pencil; never use a ballpoint pen or any kind of ink marking pen, as it may bleed through and cause a line to appear on the outside of the landau top.

Lay the top on the car and line up the center line on the top with the center line on the roof (Fig. 4-4). Position the top from front to rear making sure that the material covers both windshield posts and both rear quarters (Fig. 4-5, 4-6). Once the top is positioned, use several strips of masking tape to hold the top in place on the rear window (Fig. 4-7).

Fold the front half of the top back about four inches forward of the rear quarter window. Using a contact spray adhesive, first spray inside the rain gutters and around the windshield opening, then spray the front half of the roof completely, as though you were using paint — do not leave any areas uncovered (Fig. 4-8). Next, spray the front half of the landau top, again making sure you do not leave any areas uncovered. Always spray the metal first because the glue is not absorbed into the metal. Spraying the material last should give you an even rate of drying.

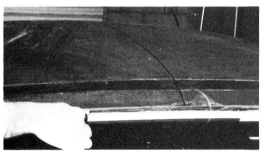

Fig. 4-3. Rear view showing center line on car roof.

Fig. 4-4. Center line on roof lines up with center line on backside of landau top.

Fig. 4-5. Position top in place to make sure material covers completely.

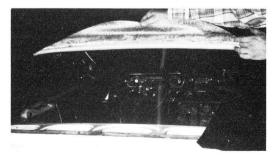

Fig. 4-6. Check center line at rear window.

You should still be able to see the pencil line on the roof and on the top. Make sure the glue is completely dry on both surfaces. If the glue is not completely dry and the top is put down, the heat from the sun will cause gases in the glue to expand and create air bubbles under the landau top.

Remove the masking tape on the forward end of the rain gutter and around the windshield (Fig. 4-9). The glue is a contact cement and must be on both surfaces in order to hold. Once the masking tape is removed the top will not stick to the window or chrome trim around the rain gutter. Touch the glue on both surfaces with your hand and, when the glue is completely dry, reach under the folded area, roll the fold forward about an inch and press down on the center line.

Now that the top is spot tacked in place, raise the folded area and pull forward while keeping the center line lined up. The masking tape on the rear window and the initial area that you glued will keep the top from shifting or moving forward. Smooth out the area from the center line to the seam on the center deck. Pull forward on the seam and smooth out the top with the palm of your hand. Go to the opposite side and do the same.

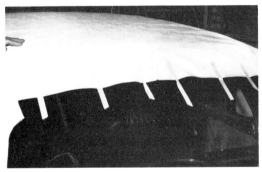

Fig. 4-7. Tape rear of landau top in position to keep it from shifting before starting to glue.

Fig. 4-8. Start gluing at front windshield.

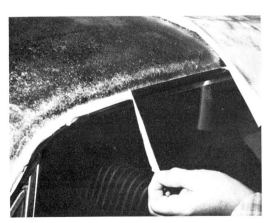

Fig. 4-9. Remove tape from front section and top will not stick where tape was removed.

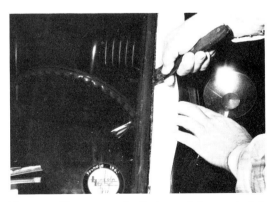

Fig. 4-10. Use a putty knife to push top material behind clips that hold chrome in place.

Next, pull forward and down at the windshield post and smooth out the wrinkles by rubbing with your hand. Make about three cuts at the curve at the upper portion of the windshield, staying at least one inch away from the rain gutter. Using your fingertips push the material down into the rain gutter; then, using a one-inch wooden paint mixer with the ends rounded off, push the material all the way down into the rain gutter.

At the upper corner of the windshield on either side, make a cut about ¼ inch away from the corner. Press the material along the edge of the window opening to form a slight crease, cut the material ½ inch longer than the crease, press the material in place around the window opening and make a small cutout around the clips that hold the stainless in place. Using a dull putty knife, push the material behind the clips and finish gluing the material between the clips (Fig. 4-10). Leave the material about 1 ½ inches long at the lower end of the windshield post (Fig. 4-11). Using a dull putty knife, push the material down under the edge of the front fender.

Remove the masking tape holding the top at the rear window and fold the top forward until you lift about ¼ inch of the glued area. Glue the rear portion of the rain gutters first, then glue the opening around the rear window. Glue the entire roof using the same procedure as the front half (Fig. 4-12). Next, glue the rear portion of the landau top, again following the same procedure as with the front half. When you have finished the gluing, remove all the masking tape (Fig. 4-13).

When the glue is dry, raise the back end of the landau top and pull it to the rear, keeping the center line lined up (Fig. 4-14). If the center line should be off a little, you can raise the top away from the glue and

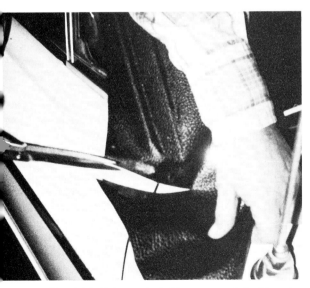

Fig. 4-11. Trim material long enough to fit under fender and windshield post.

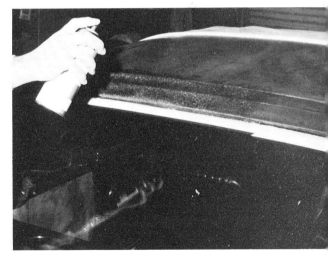

Fig. 4-12. Be sure concave area on 1965 and 1966 roofline above rear window is completely covered with glue to prevent hollow bubbles in top.

reposition it. The glue does not really hold until you rub it in place on the outside of the landau top.

Once the center line is glued down, go to the seam in the center deck and pull straight back, keeping the seam in a nice straight line. Rub the top in place from the center to the seams in the center deck. Grasp the side quarters with both hands and pull down tightly to form the rounded corners at the rear edge of the top (Fig. 4-15). Press into place and smooth out the wrinkles with your hand (Fig. 4-16). Make three cuts around the curve at the top of the rear quarter windows staying one inch away from the rain gutter.

Using the same procedure as with the front, push the material down into the rain gutter. Next, press the material against the ridge at the rear window. Trim the material ½ inch longer than the ridge and make the cutouts around the clips using the same procedure as used around the front windshield (Fig. 4-17).

On the 1964½-66 models, take extra care to press the material into the concave area just above the rear window. Make sure the material is completely down and in place, otherwise it may lift and cause a hollow area. The 1967-70 models did not have this concave area.

Fig. 4-13. Remove tape at rear quarter at chrome level.

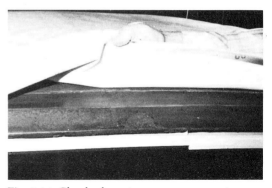

Fig. 4-14. Check glue at concave area and top to make sure glue covers both completely.

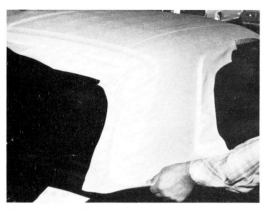

Fig. 4-15. Pull rear quarter into position and smooth out wrinkles. Glue on top will not stick where tape was removed.

Fig. 4-16. Pull material to rear and smooth out wrinkles with other hand.

Use a sharp, single-edge razor blade or razor knife to trim the excess material away from the entire rain gutter, from front to rear (Fig. 4-18). Use the dull putty knife to push the edge of the material under the chrome trim along the entire length of the rain gutter. Raise the top slightly at the bottom part of the rear quarters and locate the three holes for the chrome moldings. Use a scratch awl to punch the holes. Press the chrome molding into place. Be sure to use the soft rubber washers to prevent water from leaking around the holes. Using a 3/8 inch deep-well socket with a short extension, install the speed nuts to hold the chrome molding in place. Trim the excess material under the lower edge of the molding with a razor knife (Fig. 4-19).

On the 1964½-70 models the stainless molding around the windshield snaps in place. On the 1964½-66 models the stainless molding around the rear window snaps in place. On the 1967-68 models the lower rear window molding snaps in place but the upper and two side moldings are held in place with Phillips screws. On the 1967-70 models, place the upper and side moldings into position, locate the holes with a scratch awl and screw the molding into place (Fig. 4-20). Pull the headliner back down over the metal prongs and install the rear quarter panels, rear backrest and rear cushion.

Fig. 4-17. Trim excess material away and glue around window opening.

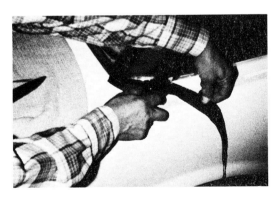

Fig. 4-19. Also cut excess away from lower chrome molding.

Fig. 4-18. Carefully remove excess material from rain gutter.

Fig. 4-20. Replace chrome trim around front and rear windows.

Chapter 5

Carpets and trunk

The four basic steps to replacing the carpeting are as follows:

1. Remove the seats, kick panels (under the dash), door sill moldings and rear quarter panels. If you have air conditioning, a console or both, you will also have to remove the console and the drain hose for the air conditioning, on the 1965 and 1966 models.
2. Remove the old carpet and padding.
3. Install the new carpet and padding.
4. Install the seats, kick panels, quarter panels and console.

Here is a list of tools and supplies you will need.

Phillips screwdriver
Straight screwdriver
Set of Allen wrenches
3/8 inch drive socket set
½ inch deep-well socket
Door handle clip puller (1965 only)
Scratch awl
Spray glue/contact trim cement

The carpet is easy to install if you follow directions; and it can be done for less than half the cost of a professional shop job.

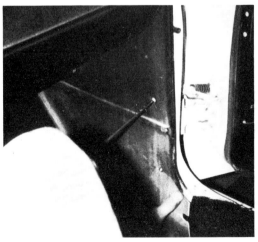

Fig. 5-1. After removing the sill plates remove both kick panels under the dash.

Fig. 5-2. On air-conditioned cars, remove the drain hose on 1965 and 1966 models.

The carpeting should be one of the last items you install. If you do the carpet before doing the headliner, the convertible top or even the dash pad, you will be getting in and out of the car and probably getting the carpet dirty. So finish your convertible top or headliner and your work on the dashboard before installing the carpet.

There are two types of Mustang carpet: sewn or molded. Ford originally used the molded carpet, so the restorer should use it also.

Many trim parts are interchangeable between the coupe and convertible. However, the carpeting, kick panels and rear quarters are different. The convertible has an additional frame member along the lower door opening, and the kick panels are shorter in height. The 1965 Mustang coupe and fastback have corresponding Naugahyde trim along the inside edge of the door sill. In the 1966 and later models the carpet goes up the door sill and under the sill molding. All convertibles have the carpet up the door sill and under the molding. (The fastback cargo section will be discussed at the end of this chapter.)

Step 1: Removing seats, kick panels, door sill moldings, rear quarter panels and console

Remove the seats as outlined earlier. Remove the two kick panels under the dash (Fig. 5-1). They are held in place with two Phillips screws. Remove the door sills and the rear quarter window regulator handles.

If your car is a 1965-66 with air conditioning, remove the drain hose from the right side of the transmission hump (Fig. 5-2).

If your car has a console without air conditioning, 1965-66 only, open the glovebox at the front end of the console and remove the two Phillips screws. Remove the three Phillips screws on each side of the console. Remove the top of the shift lever with your Allen wrench and lift the T-handle; be sure to keep the release button and T-handle

Fig. 5-3. Use Allen wrench to remove the T handle.

Fig. 5-4. Seat belts are not difficult to remove.

together (Fig. 5-3). Lift the rear of the console, disconnect the wiring and pull the console out. Remove the bracket on top of the transmission hump. Place the screws for the bracket back into the floor so they can be located after the carpet is installed.

If your car is a 1967 or 1970 with a console, the console must be removed to properly install the carpet.

On the 1968 only, use your straight screwdriver to pop the top pad cover loose, then remove it. (The 1967 does not have the padded top.) Raise the sliding glovebox door and remove the two Phillips screws. Move the shift lever to the low position and remove the shift lever cover. Take out the three Phillips screws holding the dial assembly to the console. Remove the two screws holding the radio to the rear bracket support. Remove the six screws holding the console to the floor and radio assembly (four screws on the floor and two at the radio assembly).

Remove the antenna wire, the hot lead and light wire. Raise the assembly at the rear, disconnect the feed wires to the console and pull the console out toward the rear of the car. If you don't have a console, remove the top of the T-handle with your Allen wrench. Remove the four Phillips screws around the automatic transmission selector and lift it out; leave the mounting bracket in place.

If you have a standard shift, remove the chrome plate and lift the rubber boot. Check the boot for deterioration and replace it if necessary. Remove the seat belts and check their condition (Fig. 5-4). Replace them if needed. Remove the flat-head Phillips screws holding the carpet to the floor on the front of the seat ledge (Fig. 5-5).

Step 2: Removing carpet and padding

Lift out the old carpet and padding (Fig. 5-6). The padding will be glued to the carpet and both will usually come out together, depending

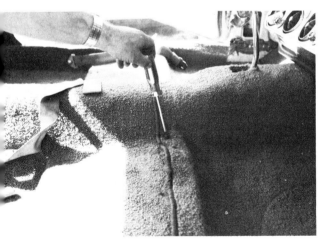

Fig. 5-5. Remove the Phillips screws holding the carpet in place.

Fig. 5-6. Old carpet must be removed.

on how badly the carpet is worn (Fig. 5-7). When the carpet is removed, lift out the insulation carefully, as it will be brittle and may break. Check the four drain plugs and check the floor for rust. Wire brush and paint the floor with a rust-inhibiting paint if needed.

Step 3: Installing new carpet and padding

Lay out your new carpeting and let it sit awhile to get out some of the wrinkles (Fig. 5-8). Replace the insulation first, front and rear. Next, lay the rear carpet in place and center it over the drive shaft hump and work it from side to side (Fig. 5-9). Lay the front carpet in place, starting at the transmission hump, and work it from side to side. On the driver's side, slide it under the gas pedal and brake pedal and line up the dimmer switch hole. Check the carpet to make sure it is centered (Fig. 5-10). When the carpet is properly centered, install the two center seat belts on the drive shaft hump.

Fig. 5-8. Lay new carpet pieces flat to remove as many wrinkles as possible.

Fig. 5-7. Also lift out the old padding.

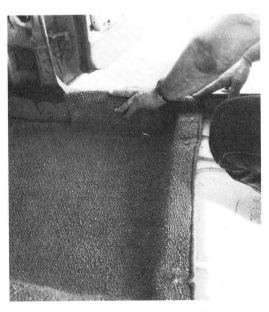

Fig. 5-9. Carpet removed and floor cleaned and ready for new carpeting.

Fig. 5-10. Lay the new carpeting in place.

Step 4: Installing seats, kick panels, door sill moldings, rear quarter panels and console

Install the rear quarter panels, rear backrest and rear cushion. If your car has the full console, 1965 and 1966, locate the two screws on the transmission hump and cut a hole around them. Install the bracket that holds the front of the console. Locate the holes and install the flat-head Phillips screws that hold the front carpet in place. Always cut a tiny hole in the carpet before using a Phillips screw, so you won't catch a thread and pull some of the loops in the carpeting. Cut holes for the seat bolts (Fig. 5-11). Locate and cut a hole inside and below the door sill for the outside half of the seat belt. Install the kick panels and door sills (Fig. 5-12). If you have a 1965 or 1966 with air conditioning, locate the drain hole and cut it out. Replace the drain hose that runs from the air conditioner to the hole in the transmission hump. Locate the holes for the seat tracks and cut them out.

Be sure to install the slotted plates between the seat track and carpeting to prevent the tracks from damaging the carpet, as the seat moves forward and backward (Fig. 5-13).

Fastback cargo area

Matching carpet kits are available for the fold-down or cargo area on the fastback. It is advisable to buy the entire carpet set when restoring your fastback. Essentially the same method of installation is used for all the fastbacks from 1965 to 1970.

There are three panels to re-cover: the flat stationary panel, the curved folding panel and the folding rear backrest support. The rear flat section has four long Phillips screws with trim washers. Remove these and take out this section. Under this section you will find two ½ inch bolts on either side. Remove these and make a note regarding how many spacers were under each side. Remove this section, leaving the hinges attached. The curved section and the flat folding section will come out as a unit. Remove the piano hinge and the latching

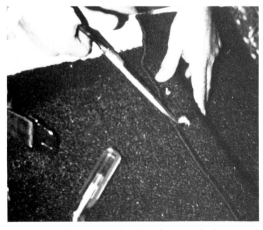

Fig. 5-11. Cut out holes for the seat bolts.

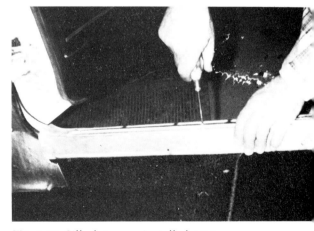

Fig. 5-12. Sill plates are installed next.

mechanism. All the chrome molding around the panels must be removed. (This is the ideal time to clean and polish the trim and lubricate the hinge and latching mechanisms.)

Lay the carpet on the panels and raise half of the carpet. Glue the metal and carpet, allow the glue to dry and set in place. Next, raise the other half and glue in the same manner. Trim the excess carpet along the edge of the metal so that the chrome moldings will fit properly. Replace the moldings and install the panels back into the car.

Trunk area

For the 1965-70 Mustangs, Ford offered a rubber mat in the small plaid or speckled pattern and a top boot storage bag for the convertible only. The NOS (new old stock) trunk mats are still available.

Since the popularity of the Mustang has grown, manufacturers have designed kits to dress up the trunk compartment. These kits include trunk mats, tire covers, jak-paks, boot storage bags and even overnight tote bags in matching materials.

Remove the spare tire. Lift out the old trunk mat. Remove the fiberboard panel on the left side of the trunk, which is held in place by a Phillips screw and flat washer. Clean the trunk area and check the drain holes. Wire brush as needed and repaint the inside of the trunk the same color as the exterior of the car.

Install the fiberboard and lay in the new trunk mat. Cut out the spare tire hold-down bracket. Put your jack in the jak-pak and place it in the position shown on the storage decal. Install the spare tire, cover it with the new tire cover and you will have a clean and low-cost trunk compartment to show your friends.

In the beginning of the book I said there were many ways in which your job could be better than a professional's. Unless you were willing to pay a very high price for your carpeting or trunk area, very few shops would take the time to check drain holes, wire brush areas and repaint as needed. Therefore, if you followed the instructions your job is better than most shop's would be.

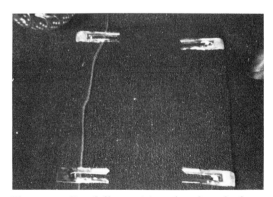

Fig. 5-13. Carefully position the slotted plates over the seat bolt holes.

Chapter 6

Convertible top

If your wife owns a convertible like my wife, Jeanie, does, you don't have to worry about installing a headliner or landau top. All you have to do is install a new convertible top. Perhaps she can help you with the project.

Here is a list of tools and supplies you will need.

Phillips screwdriver	Scratch awl
3/8 inch drive socket set	Shears
Straight screwdriver	Spray glue/contact trim cement
Diagonal side cutters	Bow locating gauge (instructions
Tack stripper	and dimensions included here)
Tack hammer	Staples
Hand stapler gun	Tacks

Installing a convertible top is probably the most rewarding of all the procedures covered here. A properly installed top puts the finishing touch on a well-restored convertible (Fig. 6-1, 6-2). To simplify instructions and not hurt the feelings of 1964½ convertible owners, I will consider their's as a 1965. The 1965-70 convertible top installation is the same. The convertible of these years came with a plastic rear window. The 1967-70 convertible had a folding glass rear window as an added option.

You can choose either version for your car. If you choose the glass window for your 1965 or 1966 you *must* also use the 1967-70 convertible top well liner. The 1965 and 1966 well liner is not large enough for the folding glass rear window.

Fig. 6-1. Before restoration.

Fig. 6-2. After a fine restoration.

After you decide on the color of the top, choose the window type, and check the pads and well liner, you are ready to strip your old convertible top.

If the car is going to be repainted, I suggest you install the top before the paint job. It is much easier to mask off the new top and repaint the car than risk scratching a new paint job while installing the top. Also, if the convertible top pads or well liner are not in excellent condition, replace them before installing the top.

The basic steps to installing your convertible top are:

1. Removing the old top, well liner and pads
2. Adjusting and preparing the frame
3. Installing the pads
4. Installing the curtain assembly and well liner
5. Installing the new top

Step 1: Removing the old top, well liner and pads

Remove the rear seat, rear backrest and both rear quarter panels as previously outlined. Cover the hood and the rear quarter area with

Fig. 6-3. *Always lay foam or a blanket on the hood to protect it while working on the convertible top.*

Fig. 6-4. *First procedure in removing the front header seal.*

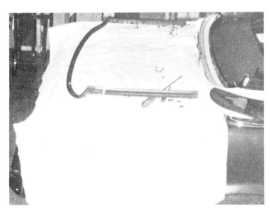

Fig. 6-5. *Only with the trunk protected, should the header seal be removed.*

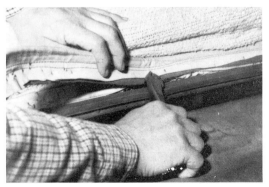

Fig. 6-6. *Remove the windlace along the front of the top header bow.*

blankets or foam (Fig. 6-3). Lower the top and remove the Phillips screws in the metal strip along the underside of the front bow. This will free the center section of the rubber header seal (Fig. 6-4). Remove the nuts holding the corners of the header seal and remove the seal (Fig. 6-5). Remove the staples in the covered windlace and remove it from the front bow (Fig. 6-6). Take out the staples holding the front of the top to the front bow and pull the material free. There is usually glue in this area so be careful not to pull the tacking strip loose. Pull the flaps loose at the front section of the side rails.

Raise the top and let it rest on the front bow without locking it into place. On the early 1965, remove the two nuts and washers on the rear

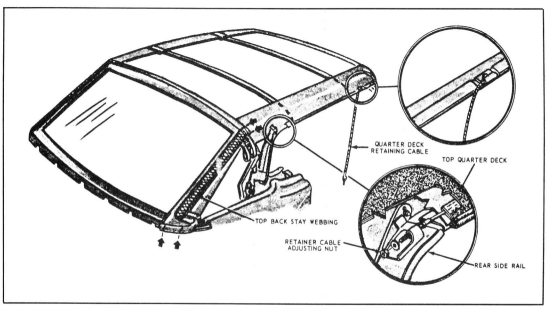

Fig. 6-7. Factory manual drawing showing the side cables and adjusting screws.

Fig. 6-8. Ball on front of 1965-70 cable.

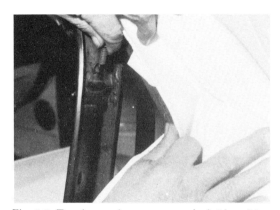

Fig. 6-9. Tension spring on rear end of side cable.

section of the hold-down side cables and slide them forward until they are free of the sleeves (Fig. 6-7). The late 1965-70 models have a cable with a ball on the front (Fig. 6-8) and a spring on the rear (Fig. 6-9). Remove the Phillips screws holding the listing retainer in the number 2 and 3 bows (Fig. 6-10). Remove the three nuts and one Phillips screw holding the rear side rail weather strips in place and take the strips off (Fig. 6-11). Pull the glued flaps loose on either side.

1965 and 1966 convertibles only

Open the trunk and disconnect the two springs holding the well liner in position (Fig. 6-12). Close the trunk and lay a blanket over the deck lid.

From inside the car, remove the Phillips screws holding the front edge of the well liner against the rear backrest support and remove the three Phillips screws on both sides of the well liner.

1967-70 convertibles only

The well liner is one piece and is held to the rear tacking strip with

Fig. 6-10. Remove number 2 and number 3 bow hold-down listing.

Fig. 6-11. Rear quarter window weather seal is removed next.

Fig. 6-12. Remove the well liner hold-down springs in trunk.

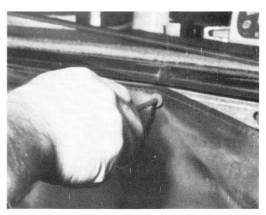

Fig. 6-13. The well liner from the rear tacking strip is removed next.

Phillips screws all the way around (Fig. 6-13). Also, there are no springs in the trunk area of the 1967-70.

On all models, 1965-70, use a 7/16 inch socket to remove all the bolts holding the rear tacking strip in place (Fig. 6-14). From outside the car, remove the two chrome ends from bow number 4, raise the edge of the wire-on and pull the staples out (Fig. 6-15). Remove the staples from the top material, both layers, and lay the top back. Take out the staples at the top edge of the rear window assembly and quarter pads and remove the top and rear window assembly, including the rear tacking strip (Fig. 6-16).

Place the entire top unit on a work table. Before removing any part of the top or rear curtain assembly from the tacking strip, use a soft lead pencil to mark the top material along the upper edge of the tacking strip (Fig. 6-17). Mark the holes or cutouts on both sides with vertical lines and mark the tacking strip at each rear corner of the top (Fig. 6-18). Also mark the old curtain with a vertical line showing where the rear corner of the top meets the rear curtain assembly. Remove the top only from

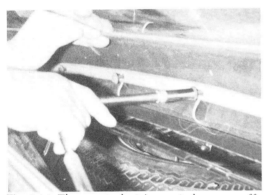

Fig. 6-14. The rear tack strip must also come off.

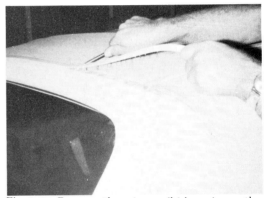

Fig. 6-15. Remove the wire-on (hide-em) over the rear window.

Fig. 6-16. Remove the upper part of the rear curtain.

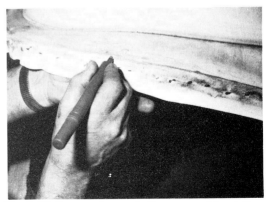

Fig. 6-17. Be sure to mark the upper side of the tack strip on the old top.

the tacking strip and mark all the holes or cutouts on the window assembly and rear quarter pads.

If your car is an early 1965, the well liner is also stapled to the tacking strip. Mark this in the same way and remove it (Fig. 6-19). If your car is a late 1965-70, the well liner is screwed to the tacking strip and is still in the car.

After you have removed the old top, rear window assembly and rear quarter pads, cut on the pencil line to remove the lower portion of the material. Also make vertical cuts for the holes or cutouts (Fig. 6-20). Lay the pieces out, preferably in the sun or at room temperature, as you will need to use them later; it will be easier if they're more pliable.

Removing the pads (as opposed to quarter pads) is next (Fig. 6-21). Remove the tape at the front edge of the pads on the number 1 bow. Ford also used Phillips screws in the number 2 and 3 bows on some cars. However, most cars had staples in these bows. Before you try to remove the Phillips screws I suggest you use some penetrating oil to

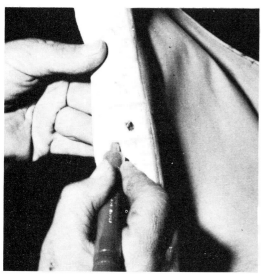

Fig. 6-18. Also mark the bolt holes in the top.

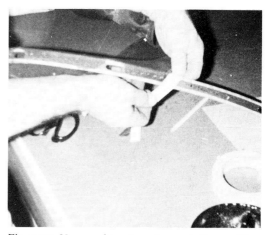

Fig. 6-19. Use masking tape to mark the position of the top pads on the rear tack strip.

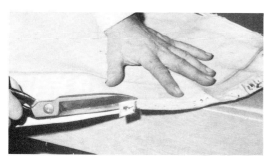

Fig. 6-20. Cut the bolt holes out of the old top so they can be used to mark the new top.

Fig. 6-21. Remove the old top pads.

loosen them (I don't know what Ford used to put them in with, but rarely do they come out easily). While the oil is working, remove the staples on the number 2, 3 and 4 bows. Then remove the Phillips screws on the number 1 bow.

Step 2: Adjusting and preparing the frame

After the top and pads are removed you should check all the tacking strips and reglue wherever necessary. This is the ideal time to check the frame for loose nuts or bolts. I also suggest repainting or touching up and lubricating where necessary.

This is the ideal time to adjust your frame. Raise both quarter windows and both door windows (Fig. 6-22). Loosen the lock nuts and move the eccentric pins with an Allen wrench to adjust the height of the intermediate side rail. After it is properly adjusted, hold the eccentric pin with the Allen wrench and tighten the locking nut. If your frame still needs adjustment go to the main pivot bracket and make the necessary modifications (Fig. 6-23).

Step 3: Installing the pads

Use the accompanying dimensions and drawings to make a bow-locating gauge for your particular year (Fig. 6-24, 6-25). Install the bow-locating gauge in position and begin installing the pads. The pads are tapered; they are wide at the rear and narrow at the front. Be sure to keep the wider part at the rear (Fig. 6-26). You will notice indentations on the bows; these are to keep the pads from bulging up on the top. Place the pad from front to rear and open it. Staple or tack the pads into place on the number 2, 3 and 4 bows (Fig. 6-27). (Use 3/8 inch brass staples or attach the pads with number 6 aluminum tacks. This prevents

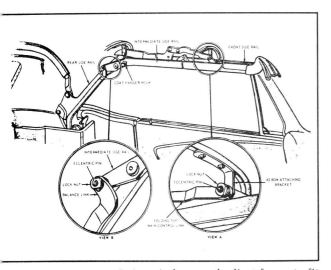

Fig. 6-22. *Raise windows and adjust frame to fit points illustrated by this factory Ford Mustang manual drawing.*

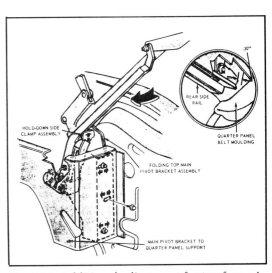

Fig. 6-23. *Additional adjustment for top frame is shown by this factory Ford Mustang manual illustration.*

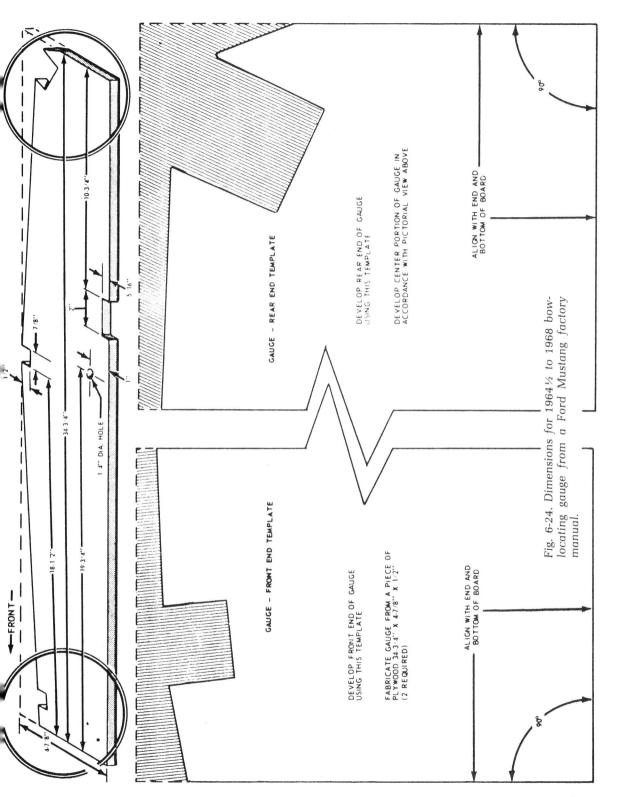

Fig. 6-24. Dimensions for 1964½ to 1968 bow-locating gauge from a Ford Mustang factory manual.

65

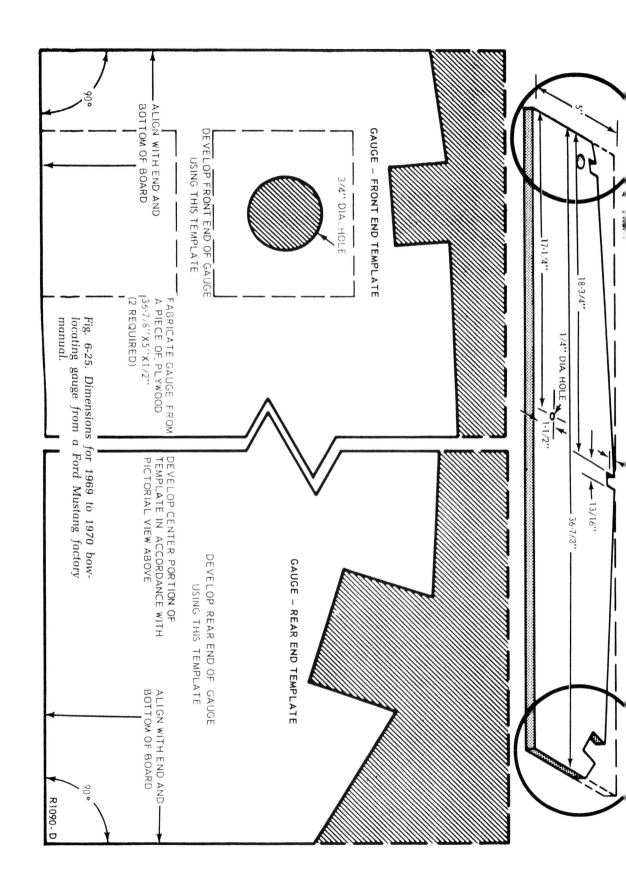

GAUGE – FRONT END TEMPLATE

3/4" DIA. HOLE

DEVELOP FRONT END OF GAUGE
USING THIS TEMPLATE

ALIGN WITH END AND
BOTTOM OF BOARD

90°

FABRICATE GAUGE FROM
A PIECE OF PLYWOOD
[35-7/8"X5"X1/2"
(2 REQUIRED)

Fig. 6-25. Dimensions for 1969 to 1970 bow-
locating gauge from a Ford Mustang factory
manual.

GAUGE – REAR END TEMPLATE

DEVELOP REAR END OF GAUGE
USING THIS TEMPLATE

DEVELOP CENTER PORTION OF
TEMPLATE IN ACCORDANCE WITH
PICTORIAL VIEW ABOVE

ALIGN WITH END AND
BOTTOM OF BOARD

90°

R1090-D

5"

17-1/4"

18-3/4"

1/4" DIA. HOLE

1-1/2"

13/16"

36-7/3"

rusting and rust marks from appearing on the top.) Keep the pads snug and replace the Phillips screws in the number 1 bow.

Spray cement on the pads and place the foam in position. Raise the lower flap and bring the upper flap on top of it. Mark a chalk line on the pad, raise the upper flap and glue the area. Bring the upper flap down and glue into place; smooth out any wrinkles.

Step 4: Installing the curtain assembly and well liner

I am now going to depart from the norm and discuss something that is just a little more work, but it really pays off in the finished product: installing the rear curtain assembly and quarter pads. (If your car is an early 1965 you will also need to install the well liner at this time.) Most trimmers will install the top at this time to save time, but I have found doing it later works the best.

Lay the new curtain assembly on a clean, soft cloth to prevent it from being scratched. Lay another soft cloth on top of the plastic or glass and lay the old curtain assembly on top of the new one.

Mark the new curtain with a soft lead pencil along the bottom edge of the old curtain assembly (Fig. 6-28). Also mark the vertical lines for the holes or cutouts. Do not cut any of these lines on the new curtain assembly yet. Find the center of the curtain assembly and mark it at the top and bottom with a light pencil line.

Measure the number 4 bow and put a center line on it. (You can use a piece of masking tape with a pencil line on it.) Put a center line on the removable tacking strip. If your car is an early 1965, first install the well liner in place.

Starting at the center, staple or tack the curtain assembly to the rear tacking strip, keeping the pencil line even with the upper edge of

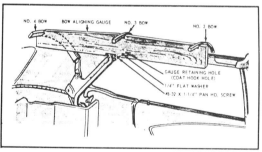

Fig. 6-26. Installation diagram from a Ford Mustang factory manual.

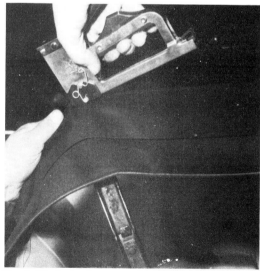

Fig. 6-27. A staple gun makes this task relatively simple.

the tacking strip and the vertical lines on either side of the holes or cutouts (Fig. 6-29). After the curtain is stapled into position, cut out the top material around the holes only; leave the excess material there.

The quarter pads are right- and left-hand pieces. To be sure they are correct, mark them the same way and install them *on top* of the rear curtain assembly. Remember, they stay in place when the rear window is lowered.

Now comes the fun. Take the curtain assembly, quarter pads and tacking strip and position them in place. (Hint: Use two scratch awls to line up the bolt holes on either end and start installing the bolts from the center out, working from side to side. Do not tighten them all the way; leave about ¼ of the thread to go.) You will notice the tacking strip can move from side to side, so keep it centered as much as possible. Lock the front bow into place; it will be loose because the rubber header seal and covered windlace are not in place. I usually lay a folded towel along the top edge of the stainless to keep it snug.

Line up the center line at the top of the rear curtain with the center line on the number 4 bow, and staple or tack the curtain in place (Fig. 6-30). Pull the curtain snug toward the end of the bow and forward, working the wrinkles out at the same time. After the curtain is fastened to the rear bow, cut away the excess material below the top ridge (Fig. 6-31). This prevents small bumps from appearing when the top is installed. Staple or tack the top of the quarter pads in place and trim the excess material the same way (Fig. 6-32).

Go back to the bolts holding the tacking strip in place and take several turns on each one; do not tighten all the way yet. This should tighten the curtain and smooth out most of the wrinkles.

Step 5: Installing the new top

Lay the old top rear quarters on the new top and line up the edges at the rear flaps that are glued over the rear quarter windows. Use a soft

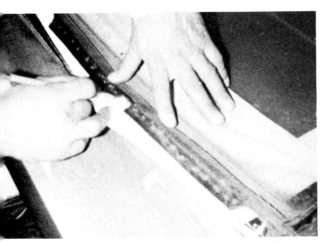

Fig. 6-28. Be sure to mark the cutouts also.

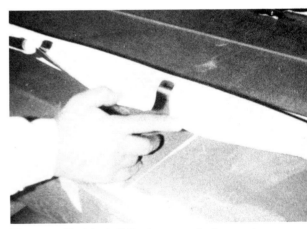

Fig. 6-29. First install the lower end of rear window on tack strip.

lead pencil to mark the upper edge of the tacking strip and the cutouts for the bolts (Fig. 6-33). Make the cutouts in the new top. Install the listing hold-downs into the listings over the number 2 and 3 bows in the new top.

Remove all the bolts holding the rear tacking strip to the body and let the strip hang loose. Lay the new top over the frame. For the early 1965, use a long piece of wire to push through the back end of the sleeve for the side cable. Pull the cable through the sleeve and slide it into place. Install the nut and washer but do not tighten all the way. The late 1965 to 1970 has the cable with the ball and spring (Fig. 6-34). Pull the spring through the sleeve and hook it into place.

For all years, line up the pencil line with the upper edge of the tacking strip, line up the cutouts in the top quarters with the holes in the

Fig. 6-30. Staple the upper end of rear window in place.

Fig. 6-31. Trim excess material at top of rear window.

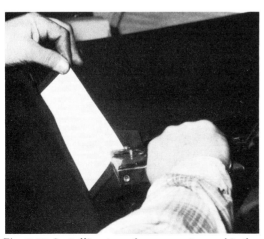

Fig. 6-32. Installing top of rear quarter pad is the next task.

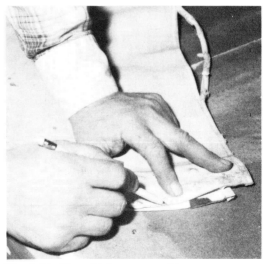

Fig. 6-33. Use old top as a guide to get proper stapling position.

tacking strip. Staple in place (Fig. 6-35). Bolt the tacking strip back to the body and leave ¼ of the thread remaining to be tightened. Glue the flap over the rear quarter windows in place and trim the excess material (Fig. 6-36). Cut the holes and install the rear side rail weather strips in place (Fig. 6-37).

Staple the valance in place over the rear window. Do not pull too high or too tight, and make sure the zipper does not show through the rear window. Check the top at the front to make sure it is properly centered.

Put the listing tie-downs into the grooves in the number 2 and number 3 bows and install the Phillips screws. Staple the seams in place on top of the valance and staple the center deck between the seams. Keep the staples in a straight line so the wire-on will evenly cover them.

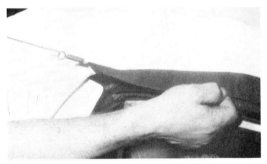

Fig. 6-34. Use a long wire with a hook to pull cable through seam.

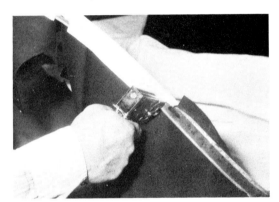

Fig. 6-35. Staple top onto tack strip.

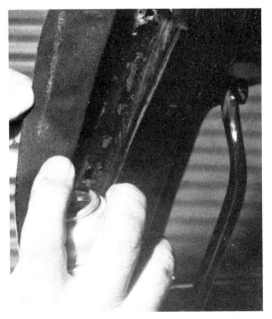

Fig. 6-36. Glue flap over rear quarter window.

Fig. 6-37. The next step is installing rear quarter window weather strip.

Pull the top forward and mark it along the front edge of the bow with a soft lead pencil (Fig. 6-38). Raise the top halfway and pull the pencil line ¼ inch over the front edge of the bow. This will make the top nice and tight after you close it.

Spray a light coat of glue on the underside of the front bow and the top material (Fig. 6-39). Glue the front of the top to the bow, keeping the ¼ inch allowance equal all the way across the bow. Staple the front of the top in place and trim the excess material (Fig. 6-40). Center the covered windlace and staple it in place, keeping the roll even with the front edge of the bow. Glue the flaps on the front edge of the side rails and cut away the excess material (Fig. 6-41). Install the side rails and header seal into place.

Lock the front bow in place. Tighten all the bolts in the rear tacking strip and the top should be nice and tight.

Fig. 6-38. Be sure to mark leading edge of top.

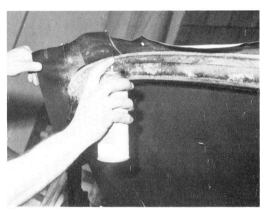

Fig. 6-39. Gluing front of top under front bow is important.

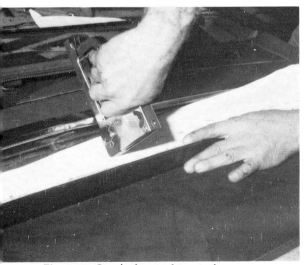

Fig. 6-40. Staple front of top to bow.

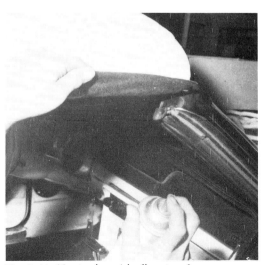

Fig. 6-41. Next, glue side flap top frame.

Clean the rain gutter below the tacking strip and check the drain holes for debris. Make sure all the excess material is in the rain gutter or water will get into the trunk area. Also check and clean the drain holes under the car, below the rear quarters.

If your car is an early 1965, install the Phillips screws at the back of the rear seat upright, and the three Phillips screws at the ends of the tacking strips. If your car is a late 1965-70, install the Phillips screws all around the tacking strip.

If your car is an early 1965, tighten the nuts on the side cable hold-downs until they are tight against the frame. Install the rear quarter panels, rear backrest and rear cushion.

Straighten the new wire-on and measure about five or six inches on either side of the center deck seam. Staple or tack the end of the wire-on in place and pull it tightly across the bow, making sure you cover the tacks or staples completely (Fig. 6-42). Staple or tack the other end in place and fill in the rest with staples or tacks. Fold the wire-on down and gently hammer it smooth. Put the ends in place and your top is completed (Fig. 6-43).

Helpful hints

Your zipper will last much longer if you use a candle to wax both sides. Always release the front of your top when lowering or raising the rear window. When driving around with your rear window down, cover it with a clean turkish towel. Never leave your window down overnight. Never leave your top down overnight.

Clean your rear window by running water over it first to remove the dirt and dust or you will scratch it. There are several good brands of plastic window cleaner; use them whenever possible. Wash your top regularly, using a mild soap.

You have worked hard installing your top and with proper care it will last a long time and you can be proud of the job. (My wife's top is four years old and still looks like new.)

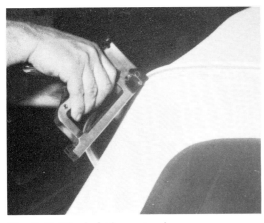

Fig. 6-42. Staple hide-em in place.

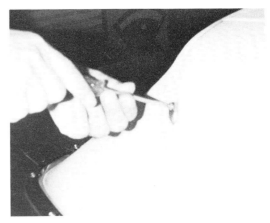

Fig. 6-43. Install the hide-em ends.

Exterior color and interior trim selections March 1964 to January 1965

EXTERIOR COLORS AND CODE
X = INTERIOR TRIM AVAILABLE

INTERIOR TRIM AND CODE
MUSTANG HARDTOP, 2+2 FASTBACK, AND CONVERTIBLE

INTERIOR TRIM AND CODE	A RAVEN BLACK	C HONEY GOLD	D DYNASTY GREEN	H CASPIAN BLUE	I CHAMPAGNE BEIGE	J RANGOON RED	K SILVER SMOKE GRAY	M WIMBLEDON WHITE	O TROPICAL TURQUOISE	P PRAIRIE BRONZE	R IVY GREEN	X VINTAGE BURGUNDY	Y SILVER BLUE	3 POPPY RED	5 TWILIGHT TURQUOISE	7 PHOENICIAN YELLOW
42 — White Vinyl with Blue Appointments				X									X			
45 — White vinyl with Red Appointments						X										
46 — White Vinyl with Black Appointments	X		X				X	X				X		X	X	X
48 — White Vinyl with Ivy Gold Appointments		X							X		X					
49 — White Vinyl with Palomino Appointments					X					X						
76 — Black Vinyl and Cloth (2+2 and Hardtop only)	X	X	X		X	X	X	X	X	X	X	X		X	X	X
79 — Palomino Vinyl and Cloth (2+2 and Hardtop only)	X								X		X					X
82 — Blue Vinyl				X					X				X			
85 — Red Vinyl	X					X	X	X								
86 — Black Vinyl	X	X	X		X	X	X	X	X	X	X	X		X	X	X
88 — Ivy Gold Vinyl	X	X							X		X	X				
89 — Palomino Vinyl	X								X	X						X**

CONVERTIBLE TOP

MAN.	POWER	COLOR	A	C	D	H	I	J	K	M	O	P	R	X	Y	3	5	7
J	1	Black	X	X	X	X	X	X	X*	X	X	X	X	X	X	X	X	X
K	2	White	X	X	X	X	X	X	X	X	X	X	X	X	X	X	X	X
L	3	Tan	X				X	X		X		X		X				X
M	4	Blue				X					X				X			

• ACCENT STRIPE

	A	C	D	H	I	J	K	M	O	P	R	X	Y	3	5	7
Black		X			X	X		X						X		X
White	X		X	X		X			X	X	X	X	X	X	X	
Red	X						X	X								

• Accent stripe is keyed to interior trim when two combinations are listed.
** Vinyl tops available on hardtop models in choice of black or white only.

Exterior color and interior trim selections February 1965 to August 1965

EXTERIOR COLOR & CODES

INTERIOR TRIM AND CODE		Code	A RAVEN BLACK	C HONEY GOLD	D DYNASTY GREEN	H CASPIAN BLUE	I CHAMPAGNE BEIGE	J RANGOON RED	K SILVER SMOKE GRAY	M WIMBLEDON WHITE	O TROPICAL TURQUOISE	P PRAIRIE BRONZE	R IVY GREEN	X VINTAGE BURGUNDY	Y SILVER BLUE	3 POPPY RED	5 TWILIGHT TURQUOISE	7 PHOENICIAN YELLOW	V SUNLIGHT YELLOW	F ARCADIAN BLUE	8 SPRINGTIME YELLOW
STANDARD BUCKET SEATS	Blue	22				X				X					X					X	
	Red	25	X					X	X	X											
	Black	26	X	X			X	X	X	X	X	X	X	X		X	X	X	X		X
	Aqua	27	X							X	X						X				
	Palamino	29	X			X	X	X		X	X	X		Y				X	X		X
	Parchment w/Blue Appointments	D2				X				X					X					X	
	Parchment w/Burgundy Appointments	D3								X					X						
	Parchment w/Red Appointments	D5	X					X		X											
	Parchment w/Black Appointments	D6	X	X	X		X	X	X	X	X	X			X		X		X	X	X
	Parchment w/Aqua Appointments	D7								X	X										
	Parchment w/Ivy Gold Appointments	D8	X	X						X			X								
	Parchment w/Palomino Appointments	D9						X		X		X			X		X	X	X	X	X
INTERIOR DECOR GROUP OPTION	Blue and White	62				X				X					X					X	
	Red	65	X					X	X	X											
	Black	66	X	X	X		X	X	X	X	X	X	X	X		X	X	X	X		X
	Aqua and White	67	X							X											
	Ivy Gold and White	68	X	X						X			X								
	Palamino	69	X					X		X	X	X		Y		X	X	X	X		X
	Parchment w/Blue Appointments	F2				X				X					X					X	
	Parchment w/Burgundy Appointments	F3								X					X						
	Parchment w/Emberglo Appointments	F4								X									X		X
	Parchment w/Red Appointments	F5	X					X		X											
	Parchment w/Black Appointments	F6					X	X	X	X	X	X	X	X		X	X	X	X		X
	Parchment w/Aqua Appointments	F7	X							X											
	Parchment w/Ivy Gold Appointments	F8	X	X						X			X								
	Parchment w/Palomino Appointments	F9						X		X		X			X		X	X	X	X	X
BENCH SEAT OPTION	Blue	32				X				X					X					X	
	Red	35	X					X	X	X											
	Black	36	X	X	X		X	X	X	X	X	X	X	X		X	X	X	X		X
	Palamino	39	X					X	X	X	X	X		Y				X	X		X
	Parchment w/Blue Appointments	C2				X				X					X					X	
	Parchment w/Burgundy Appointments	C3								X					X						
	Parchment w/Emberglo Appointments	C4								X									X		X
	Parchment w/Black Appointments	C6		X	X		X	X	X	X	X	X	X	X		X		X	X		X
	Parchment w/Aqua Appointments	C7	X							X											
	Parchment w/Ivy Gold Appointments	C8	X	X						X			X								
	Parchment w/Palomino Appointments	C9						X		X		X			X		X	X	X	X	X

STRIPES W/ACCENT OR GT GROUP OPTION*

	A	C	D	H	I	J	K	M	O	P	R	X	Y	3	5	7	V	F	8
Black		X			X	X	X	X	X	X			X		X	X	X	X	X
White	X		X	X	X			X		X	X	X	X	X	X				
Dark Red	X					X	X												
Dark Blue								X											

CONVERTIBLE TOP

	Manual	Power	A	C	D	H	I	J	K	M	O	P	R	X	Y	3	5	7	V	F	8
Black	J	1	X	X	X	X	X	X	X	X	X	X	X	X	X	X	X	X	X	X	X
White	K	2	X	X	X	X	X	X	X	X	X	X	X	X	X	X	X	X	X	X	X
Tan	L	3	X				X	X		X		X			X			X	X		X

*Stripe color is keyed to interior trim when more than one option is listed.
Vinyl tops available on hardtop models in choice of black or white only.

**Bench seat option not available with interior decor option.

Exterior color and interior trim selections 1966

INTERIOR TRIM AND CODE — ALL-VINYL	A Raven Black	F Arcadian Blue	H Sahara Beige	K Nightmist Blue	M Wimbledon White	P Antique Bronze	R Ivy Green	T Candyapple Red	U Tahoe Turquoise	V Emberglo	X Vintage Burgundy	Y Silver Blue	Z Sauterne Gold	4 Silver Frost	5 Signalflare Red	8 Springtime Yellow
STANDARD BUCKET SEATS																
Blue 22	O	X		X	X							X		O		
Red 25	X				X			X			X			X	X	
Black 26	X	O	X	O	X	X	X	X	X	O	X	O	X	X	X	X
Aqua 27	X				X				X							
Parchment w/Blue Appointments D2		X		X								X				
Parchment w/Burgundy Appointments D3								X			X				O	
Parchment w/Emberglo Appointments D4										X						
Parchment w/Black Appointments D6	X															X
Parchment w/Aqua Appointments D7									X							
Parchment w/Ivy Gold Appointments D8						X								O		
Parchment w/Palomino Appointments D9			X		X	X										
INTERIOR DECOR GROUP OPTION BUCKET SEATS																
Blue and White 62	O	X		X	X							X		O		
Emberglo and Parchment 64	X		X		X						X					
Red 65	X				X			X			X			X	X	
Black 66	X	O	X	O	X	X	X	X	X	O	X	O	X	X	X	X
Aqua and White 67	X				X				X							
Ivy Gold and White 68	X				X		X						X			
Parchment w/Blue Appointments F2		X		X								X				
Parchment w/Burgundy Appointments F3								X			X				O	
Parchment w/Emberglo Appointments F4										X						
Parchment w/Black Appointments F6	X															X
Parchment w/Aqua Appointments F7									X							
Parchment w/Ivy Gold Appointments F8						X								O		
Parchment w/Palomino Appointments F9			X		X	X										
***BENCH SEAT OPTION**																
Blue 32	O	X		X	X							X				
Red 35	X				X			X			X			X	X	
Black 36	X	O	X	O	X	X	X	X	X	O	X	O	X	X	X	X
Parchment w/Blue Appointments C2		O		O									O			
Parchment w/Burgundy Appointments C3								X			X				O	
Parchment w/Emberglo Appointments C4										X						
Parchment w/Black Appointments C6	X															X
Parchment w/Aqua Appointments C7									X							
Parchment w/Ivy Gold Appointments C8						X								O		
Parchment w/Palomino Appointments C9			X		X	X										
§STRIPES W/ACCENT GROUP OPTION																
Black 1		X	X		X	X		▲X		▲X			X	X		X
White 2	X			X		X	X	X	X		X	X	X		X	
Red 3	†X				†X										†X	
STRIPES W/GT OPTION																
Black			X			X		▲X			X		X	X		X
White	X			X	X	♦X	X	X	X		X	♦X	X		X	
Red	†X				#X										†X	
Dark Blue		X			#X											

NOTE: Convertible Tops and Vinyl Roof Option for Hardtop are available in Black or White with all Exterior Colors.
*Not available with 2+2 Fastback   ‡Red Stripe only with Red Interior, Dark Blue Stripe only with Blue Interior.
§Not available in combination with GT option   ♦White Stripe only with Parchment Interior
†Red Stripe only with Red Interior
▲Black Stripe only with Black Interior

X = Recommended   O = Also Available

INTERIOR TRIM AND CODE ALL-VINYL		A Raven Black	B Frost Turquoise	E Beige Mist	I Lime Gold	K Nightmist Blue	M Wimbledon White	Q Brittany Blue	T Candyapple Red	V Burnt Amber	W Clearwater Aqua	X Vintage Burgundy	Y Dark Moss Green	Z Sauterne Gold	4 Silver Frost	6 Pebble Beige	8 Springtime Yellow
STANDARD BUCKET SEATS																	
Black	2A	X	X	X	X	X	X	X	X	X	X	X	X	X	X	X	X
Blue	2B	X				X	X	X							X		
Red	2D	X					X		X			X			X		
Saddle	2F	X		X						X			X			X	X
Ivy Gold	2G	X				X	X							X	X		
Aqua	2K	X	X				X				X						
Parchment	2U	X	O	X	O	O	X	O	X	X	O	X	X	O		X	X
INTERIOR DECOR GROUP OPTION BUCKET SEATS																	
Black	6A	X	X	X	X	X	X	X	X	X	X	X	X	X	X	X	X
Blue	6B	X				X	X	X							X		
Red	6D	X					X		X			X			X		
Saddle	6F	X		X			X			X			X			X	X
Ivy Gold	6G	X				X	X							X	X		
Aqua	6K	X	X				X				X						
Parchment	6U	X	O	X	O	O	X	O	X	X	O	X	X	O		X	X
FULL-WIDTH SEAT OPTION (Hardtop and Convertible)																	
Black	4A	X	X	X	X	X	X	X	X	X	X	X	X	X	X	X	X
Parchment	4U	X	O	X	O	O	X	O	X	X	O	X	X	O		X	X
STANDARD BUCKET SEATS W/COMFORT-WEAVE OPTION (Hardtop and 2 + 2 Fastback)																	
Black	7A	X	X	X	X	X	X	X	X	X	X	X	X	X	X	X	X
Parchment	7U	X	O	X	O	O	X	O	X	X	O	X	X	O		X	X
INTERIOR DECOR GROUP OPTION W/COMFORT-WEAVE SEAT OPTION (Hardtop and 2 + 2 Fastback)																	
Black	5A	X	X	X	X	X	X	X	X	X	X	X	X	X	X	X	X
Parchment	5U	X	O	X	O	O	X	O	X	X	O	X	X	O		X	X
ACCENT PAINT STRIPE OPTION																	
Black			X	X	X	X			#X	X					X	X	X
White		X				X		X	X		X	X	X				
Red		#X					*X								*X		
STRIPES W/GT OPTION																	
Black			X	X	X	X			#X	X					X	X	X
White		X				X		X	X		X	X	X				
Red		*X					*X								*X		
Medium Blue							†X										

CONVERTIBLE TOPS—Available in black or white with all exterior colors.
HARDTOP VINYL ROOF OPTION—Available in black or pastel parchment with all exterior colors.
TWO-TONE REAR BODY PANEL OPTION—Available in dark gray metallic with all exterior colors.

X—Recommended.   O—Also Available.   *Red stripe only with red interior.
#Black stripe only with black interior.   †Medium blue stripe only with blue interior.

Exterior color and interior trim selections 1968

INTERIOR TRIM AND CODE		A — Raven Black	B — Royal Maroon	D — Acapulco Blue	F — Gulfstream Aqua	I — Lime Gold	M — Wimbledon White	N — Diamond Blue	O — Sea Foam Green	Q — Brittany Blue	R — Highland Green	T — Candyapple Red	U — Tahoe Turquoise	X — Presidential Blue	W — Meadowlark Yellow	Y — Sunlit Gold	6 — Pebble Beige
STANDARD BUCKET—ALL VINYL																	
Black	2A, 6A*	X	X	X	X	X	X	X	X	X	X	X	X	X	X	X	X
Blue	2B, 6B*	X		X			X	X		X				X			
Dark Red	2D, 6D*	X	X				X	X				X					
Saddle	2F, 6F*	X					X				X				X		X
Ivy Gold	2G, 6G*	X				X	X		X		X						
Aqua	2K, 6K*	X			X		X						X				
Parchment	2U, 6U*	X	X	O	O	O	X		O	O	X	X	O	O	X	X	X
Nugget Gold	2Y, 6Y*	X					X	X			X				X	X	
FULL-WIDTH SEAT OPTION WITH COMFORT-WEAVE VINYL (Hardtop and 2+2 Fastback)																	
Black	8A, 9A*	X	X	X	X	X	X	X	X	X	X	X	X	X	X	X	X
Blue	8B, 9B*	X		X			X	X		X				X			
Dark Red	8D, 9D*	X	X				X	X				X					
Parchment	8U, 9U*	X	X	O	O	O	X		O	O	X	X	O	O	X	X	X
BUCKET SEAT WITH COMFORT-WEAVE VINYL OPTION (Hardtop and 2+2 Fastback)																	
Black	7A, 5A*	X	X	X	X	X	X	X	X	X	X	X	X	X	X	X	X
Blue	7B, 5B*	X		X			X	X		X				X			
Dark Red	7D, 5D*	X	X				X	X				X					
Parchment	7U, 5U*	X	X	O	O	O	X		O	O	X	X	O	O	X	X	X
ACCENT PAINT STRIPE OPTION																	
Black							X	X[3]	X	X		X[6]			X	X	X
White		X[2]	X[7]	X	X					X	X[2]	X	X	X			
Red							X[4]	X[4]									
Blue							X[5]	X[5]									

CONVERTIBLE TOPS—Available in black or parchment with all exterior colors.
HARDTOP VINYL ROOF OPTION—Available in black or parchment with all exterior colors.

X—Recommended   O—Also Available
*Used when the Decor Group is ordered.
[1] Body side accent stripes are optional at extra cost on all models. "GT" single paint stripe at character line is optional at extra cost. For the "GT" Group, dual tapered "C" shape or triple lower rocker stripes are standard equipment.
[2] Gold tape stripe also used with black, saddle, parchment, and nugget gold interiors.
[3] Gold tape stripe also used with saddle and nugget gold interiors.
[4] With red interior only.
[5] With blue interior only.
[6] With black interior only.
[7] Gold tape stripe also used with black or parchment interiors.

Exterior color and interior trim selections 1969

Charts shown reflect the color and trim combinations. Exterior colors and codes are in the first chart and the trim combinations follow. Colors and codes referenced are the same as those shown in your Color and Upholstery Book.

EXTERIOR COLORS AND CODES

Color	Code	Color	Code
Raven Black	A	Winter Blue	P
Royal Maroon	B	Champagne Gold	S
Black Jade	C	Candyapple Red	T
Acapulco Blue	D	Meadowlark Yellow	W
Aztec Aqua	E	Indian Fire	Y
Gulfstream Aqua	F	New Lime	2
Lime Gold	I	Silver Jade	4
Wimbledon White	M	Pastel Gray	6

HARDTOP, SPORTSROOF AND CONVERTIBLE
ALL-VINYL BUCKET SEAT

Interior Trims		Exterior Color
Color	Code	Availability Codes
Black	2A	All
Blue	2B	A D M P 6
Red	2D	A B M T 6
Ivy Gold	2G	A C I M W 2 6
Nugget Gold	2Y	A C M S W

HARDTOP, SPORTSROOF AND CONVERTIBLE
COMFORTWEAVE KNITTED VINYL OPTIONAL HI-BACK BUCKET SEAT

Interior Trims			Exterior Color
Color	Code	Code*	Availability Codes
Black	4A	DA	All
Red	4D	DD	A B M T 6
White	—	DW	All (except 6)

*RPO seat with Interior Decor Group option.

HARDTOP AND SPORTSROOF
COMFORTWEAVE KNITTED VINYL DELUXE BUCKET SEAT

Interior Trims		Exterior Color
Color	Code	Availability Codes
Black	5A	All
Blue	5B	A D M P 6
Red	5D	A B M T 6
Ivy Gold	5G	A C I M W 2 6
White	5W	All (except 6)
Nugget Gold	5Y	A C M S W

HARDTOP
COMFORTWEAVE KNITTED VINYL BENCH SEAT

Interior Trims			Exterior Color
Color	Code	Code*	Availability Codes
Black	8A	9A	All
Blue	8B	9B	A D M P 6
Red	8D	9D	A B M T 6
Nugget Gold	8Y	9Y	A C M S W

*RPO seat with Interior Decor Group option.

CONVERTIBLE
DELUXE ALL-VINYL BUCKET SEAT

Interior Trims		Exterior Color
Color	Code	Availability Codes
Black	7A	All
Blue	7B	A D M P 6
Red	7D	A B M T 6
Ivy Gold	7G	A C I M W 2 6
White	7W	All (except 6)
Nugget Gold	7Y	A C M S W

GRANDÉ HARDTOP
LUXURY CLOTH AND VINYL

Interior Trims		Exterior Color
Color	Code	Availability Codes
Black	1A	All
Blue	1B	A D M P 6
Ivy Gold	1G	A C I M W 2 6
Nugget Gold	1Y	A C M S W

MACH I SPORTSROOF
COMFORTWEAVE KNITTED VINYL MACH I BUCKET SEAT

Interior Trims		Exterior Color
Color	Code	Availability Codes
Black	3A	All
Red	3D	A B M T 6
White	3W	All (except 6)

TAPE STRIPE CODES/AVAILABILITY

Color	Code
Black*	1
White	2
Red	3
Gold*	8

EXTERIOR COLOR **	INTERIOR TRIM COLOR					
	Black	Blue	Red	Ivy Gold	Nugget Gold	White
Raven Black	8	2	3	8	8	2
(Grandé)		8				
(Mach I)	3					
Royal Maroon	8		8			2
(Mach I)						8
Black Jade	8		8	8		2
(Mach I)						8
Acapulco Blue	1	2				2
(Grandé)		1				1
Aztec Aqua	1					1
Gulfstream Aqua	2					2
(Mach I)	1					1
Lime Gold	1			1		1
Wimbledon White	1	1	3	8	8	1
Winter Blue	1	2				2
(Mach I)						1
Champagne Gold	1				1	1
Candyapple Red	1		6			2
(Grandé)			8			8
Meadowlark Yellow	1			8	8	1
Indian Fire	1					2
(Mach I)						8
New Lime	1			1		1
Silver Jade						1
Pastel Grey	1	1	3	1		

*On Grandé, tape stripes are two-tone. Black is with Gold; Gold is with White.

**Grandé and Mach I availability is shown in ( ) only when different from general availability.

CONVERTIBLE TOP COLOR COMBINATIONS

CONVERTIBLE TOP		Exterior Color
Color	Code	Availability
Black	1	All
White	2	All

VINYL ROOF COVERING

Vinyl roofs are available in black (Code 2) or white (Code 4) on all hardtops.

Exterior color and interior trim selections 1970

Charts shown reflect the color and trim combinations. Exterior colors and codes are in the first chart and the trim combinations follow. Colors and codes referenced are the same as those shown in your Color and Upholstery Book.

EXTERIOR COLORS AND CODES

Color	Code	Color	Code
Black	A	Medium Gold Metallic	S
Dark Ivy Green Metallic	C	Red	T
Bright Yellow	D	Vermilion	1
Medium Lime Metallic	G	Light Ivy Yellow	2
Bright Gold Metallic	K	Bright Blue Metallic	6
White	M	Grabber Blue	J9
Pastel Blue	N	Grabber Orange	U9
Medium Blue Metallic	Q	Grabber Green	Z9

HARDTOP, SPORTSROOF AND CONVERTIBLE
ALL-VINYL

Interior Trims		Exterior Color Availability Codes
Color	Code	
Black	BA	All
Blue	BB	A M N Q 6
Vermilion	BE	A M T 1
Ginger	BF	A C K M S 2
Ivy	BG	A C G M 2
White	BW	All

CONVERTIBLE
OPTIONAL COMFORTWEAVE KNITTED VINYL

Interior Trims		Exterior Color Availability Codes
Color	Code	
Black	EA	All
Blue	EB	A M N Q 6
Ivy	EG	A C G M 2
White	—	All

HARDTOP AND SPORTSROOF
OPTIONAL COMFORTWEAVE KNITTED VINYL

Interior Trims		Exterior Color Availability Codes
Color	Code	
Black	TA	All
Blue	TB	A M N Q 6
Ivy	TG	A C G M 2
White	TW	All

HARDTOP AND SPORTSROOF
BLAZER STRIPE CLOTH AND VINYL

Interior Trims		Exterior Color Availability Codes
Color	Code	
Vermilion	UE	A M T 1
Ginger	UF	A C K M S 2

CONVERTIBLE
BLAZER STRIPE CLOTH AND VINYL

Interior Trims		Exterior Color Availability Codes
Color	Code	
Vermilion	CE	A M T 1
Ginger	CF	A C K M S 2

GRANDÉ HARDTOP
HOUNDSTOOTH CLOTH AND VINYL

Interior Trims		Exterior Color Availability Codes
Color	Code	
Black	AA	All
Blue	AB	A M N Q 6
Vermilion	AE	A M T 1
Ginger	AF	A C K M S 2
Ivy	AG	A C G M 2

MACH I SPORTSROOF
COMFORTWEAVE KNITTED VINYL

Interior Trims		Exterior Color Availability Codes
Color	Code	
Black	3A	All
Blue	3B	A M N Q 6
Ivy	3G	A C G M 2
White	3W	All
Vermilion	3E	A M T 1
Ginger	3F	A C K M S 2

GRANDÉ TAPE STRIPE CODES/AVAILABILITY

Color	Code
Black	B
White	W
Red	R
Gold	G

EXTERIOR COLOR	INTERIOR TRIM COLOR				
	Black	Blue	Vermilion	Ginger	Ivy
Black	G	W	R	G	G
Dark Ivy Green Metallic	G			G	G
Bright Yellow	B				
Medium Lime Metallic	B				B
Bright Gold Metallic	B			B	
White	B	B	R	B	B
Pastel Blue	B	B			
Medium Blue Metallic	B	B			
Medium Gold Metallic	B			B	
Red	W		W		
Vermilion	B		B		
Light Ivy Yellow	B			B	B
Bright Blue Metallic	W	W			
Grabber Blue	B				
Grabber Orange	B				
Grabber Green	B				

CONVERTIBLE TOP COLOR COMBINATIONS

CONVERTIBLE TOP		Exterior Color Availability
Color	Code	
Black	1	All
White	2	All

VINYL ROOF AVAILABILITY

Roof Color	Full Roof (HT and Grandé)	Landau Roof (Grandé only)	Exterior Trim	Interior Trim
Black Levant	1	S	All	All
White Levant	2	T	All*	All
Blue Houndstooth	C	—	MNQ	BB1W
Blue Houndstooth	C	—	AM	B1
Green Houndstooth	E	—	CG2	B1W
Green Houndstooth	E	—	AM	1
Saddle Kiwi	6	—	ACKMS	G

*NA with N-Pastel Blue